Praise for *Building a Curious School*

"This is an important book. Although many authors have written about curiosity as a powerful tool in the learning process, none, to my knowledge, have approached the topic with the clarity provided by Bryan Goodwin. Much more than a collection of instructional strategies, this book lays out a vision as to the way schools can and should be approached to stimulate curiosity as a natural part of the teaching and learning process."

—Robert J. Marzano
Cofounder and CAO, Marzano Resources
Cofounder and Strategic Advisor, Marzano Research

"This intriguing read is thought-provoking, relevant, and practical all at once. Bryan Goodwin researches the strong links between curiosity and longevity, curiosity and student engagement, and curiosity and strong instruction in the classroom. A powerful must-read for all educators who want learning to be not only lively but also impactful and meaningful for every student."

—Lyn Sharratt
Internship Supervisor
Ontario Institute for Studies in Education
University of Toronto, Canada

"Bryan Goodwin reminds us that wonder and curiosity are natural forces in all of us that need to be rekindled in our schools if we are to make learning engaging and meaningful."

—Harvey Silver
Education Coach and Consultant
Co-founder of Silver Strong & Associates
Co-author, *The Core Six, The Strategic Teacher,* and
Tools for a Successful School Year

"We have come to recognize that in education the key to success lies within the context of collaborative inquiry as a means for questioning, learning, and improving. Bryan Goodwin has gone beyond this general viewpoint and defined the secret ingredient

for success among students, teachers, schools and organizations; curiosity. *Building a Curious School* provides the research, reflective activities and tools that are needed to bring curiosity to life in our schools."

—Jay Westover
Co-founder and Chief Learning Officer, InnovateEd
Author, *Districts on the Move*

Building a Curious School is a compelling call to action. With solid research, powerful examples, and practical guidance, Bryan Goodwin explains why schools must respect and help develop children's curiosity as well as what educators can do to nurture curiosity in children. An excellent read for all interested in becoming more curious and helping others to become curious.

—Yong Zhao
Foundation Distinguished Professor
School of Education
University of Kansas

BUILDING A

CURIOUS
SCHOOL

BUILDING A CURIOUS SCHOOL

RESTORE THE JOY THAT BROUGHT YOU TO SCHOOL

BRYAN GOODWIN

FOREWORD BY SALOME THOMAS-EL

A JOINT PUBLICATION

FOR INFORMATION:

Corwin

A SAGE Company

2455 Teller Road

Thousand Oaks, California 91320

(800) 233-9936

www.corwin.com

SAGE Publications Ltd.

1 Oliver's Yard

55 City Road

London, EC1Y 1SP

United Kingdom

SAGE Publications India Pvt. Ltd.

B 1/I 1 Mohan Cooperative Industrial Area

Mathura Road, New Delhi 110 044

India

SAGE Publications Asia-Pacific Pte. Ltd.

18 Cross Street #10-10/11/12

China Square Central

Singapore 048423

Printed in the United States of America.

ISBN 978-1-0718-1392-8

Publisher: Arnis Burvikovs

Acquisitions Editor: Ariel Curry

Development Editor: Desirée A. Bartlett

Associate Editor: Eliza B. Erickson

Associate Content Development Editor: Jessica Vidal

Production Editor: Tori Mirsadjadi

Copy Editor: Amy Hanquist Harris

Typesetter: Hurix Digital

Proofreader: Eleni Maria Georgiou

Indexer: Mary Mortensen

Cover Designer: Gail Buschman

Marketing Manager: Sharon Pendergast

This book is printed on acid-free paper.

20 21 22 23 24 10 9 8 7 6 5 4 3 2 1

CONTENTS

FOREWORD

by Salome Thomas-EL

I am writing the foreword to this important book after spending a Saturday morning with about 100 students and teachers in our school's Saturday Academy program. This program is voluntary for students and allows them to work on reading and writing skills with some time built in for fun activities to explore their critical thinking, and some exercise too. It helps that we provide them with pizza for lunch before they journey back home for the weekend, I'm sure. Watching those students and teachers revel in the company of one another, strengthen the relationships they develop during the week, and engage in rigorous and fun activities, makes me feel very good as a teacher, principal and father. Finding innovative ways to encourage students and teachers to explore their curiosity and the wonders of learning should be on the minds of principals and school leaders around the world.

As a teacher and principal in inner-city schools for over thirty years, I have always felt that we focused on teaching students to see the turns in life, and not enough on thinking about what might be around those turns. In *Building a Curious School*, Bryan Goodwin has provided a road map for educators who are interested in helping their students become independent thinkers and to advocate for themselves. My mission during my entire career has been to provide students with a culture that fosters critical thinking and problem-solving skills and allows them to find success in school and in life. I wanted the students to become resilient and comfortable with their own struggles, failures, and victories, and to explore their curiosities about school and life. As teachers and administrators, it is important for us to build curious cultures in our classrooms and schools so that we foster those powerful relationships that we know can develop when we care and love one another.

In this thought-provoking book, teachers, principals and parents can read about the importance of teaching students about service and making meaningful contributions to their communities. Those who know and have met me over the years are aware that being curious about our student's lives is one of my Four C's of school success. We can learn so much about our students and their communities through our own curiosity, care and concern. Once we are aware of the needs of our students inside and outside of school, we can become so much better at building and developing strong relationships that will sustain our children for years to come. Curious teachers and principals become better learners and must always place a priority on developing learning cultures instead of teaching cultures. Educators and parents who are curious about children are so much more likely to be engaged, supportive, understanding and successful. Successful schools are filled with curious kids and adults.

In *Building a Curious School*, educators and parents can learn practical ways to instill curiosity in their classrooms, schools and homes. We also learn that building strong relationships with our children requires us to establish cultures that foster critical thinking, risk-taking and curiosity. Children ask hundreds of questions each day at home before they begin school, but once they arrive to us, they are told to be quiet and to raise their hands if they wish to speak. Yes, children need to learn manners but we must also nurture their curiosity and encourage our students to ask more questions for deeper learning and understanding. Testing children on a regular basis won't make them smarter, but fostering curiosity, engagement, rigor and joy each day will!

If your goal is to inspire parents and students to knock down the doors to get into your school instead of to get out, then this book is a must-read for you and your colleagues. Building schools that attract parents will require us to become more curious about their children and to spark that same curiosity in them. Making connections and developing long-lasting relationships with our students and their families will become the key to their success and resilience. That happens when we become curious educators who realize the tremendous impact we have on our students. This is even more important for families living in struggling communities.

We can no longer afford to be tiny sparks for our kids! Increasing the curiosity of our students will lead to them becoming better citizens who work toward building a better world. With an increased focus on social emotional learning and equity for all students, schools can become the kinds of places kids look forward to attending each day, even on an occasional Saturday.

PREFACE

This book is written for any educator who has ever looked out across your classroom, school, or district and had a nagging feeling something's gone missing. Maybe it was once there, long ago, but has since been buried under an avalanche of unfunded mandates, unrelenting pressures, and unintended consequences of policies landing on the doorstep of your school or classroom from far off places. Or maybe you've *never* really felt it at all, even though it's what drew you to the profession in the first place.

Nonetheless, you have a hunch that what's missing could be restored in our schools—likely because you've seen it happening everywhere *outside of school*—when children run excitedly across a museum to marvel at an exhibit, search for tadpoles in a summertime creek, take something apart to see how it works, or listen in rapt attention when grandparents share stories from a distant homeland or days gone by. In those moments, you've seen learning in its purest, deepest, and most powerful form—when kids experience the joy of wondering and wandering, chasing horizons, making discoveries, expanding their minds, solving puzzles, and getting to the bottom of mysteries. In a word, when they're *curious*.

In many ways, this book reflects my own long journey that began years ago when, as a teacher, I had a similar nagging feeling that something wasn't quite right in my classroom. I'd hope to inspire passion for learning among my students (picturing myself like Robin Williams standing on a desk in *Dead Poet's Society*, intoning, "Captain, my Captain!"). But when I looked around, I couldn't shake the feeling that my students were just checking boxes, jumping through hoops, and scoring points for a grade so they could move onto the next class and do it all over again.

At first, I wasn't sure exactly what was wrong or what to do about it. All I knew was I couldn't shake the feeling that something was amiss in our education system. So I kept exploring and poking around for the answer—something I've had the unusual luxury of doing while spending two decades working at and eventually being honored to serve as the leader of McREL International, a nonprofit organization that for 50-plus years has helped educators translate research into solutions for their most pressing problems of practice.

This book reflects many treasures I've accumulated along the way—insights gleaned from hundreds of scientific studies and, more importantly, from real-life experiences of educators like you, who asked and found answers to their questions about how to restore the joy of learning to their schools and classrooms. That said, it doesn't offer a simplistic, cookie-cutter recipe for creating a curious school. That's because there is no such recipe. While curious schools share many similar elements and often follow similar guiding principles, as you'll see, they each experience their own journeys of exploration and discovery and thus seldom arrive at exactly the same spot.

So what you'll find in these pages is less of a checklist and more of a travel guide for your journey toward curiosity—one that invites you to explore and make your own discoveries. The first waypoint of this journey, captured in Part I of this book, unpacks the many facets of curiosity and ways we and our students demonstrate curiosity. It also explores what research and brain science tell us about the powerful effects of curiosity on learning and long-term memory.

In Part II, we'll explore together how current approaches to teaching often quash curiosity in the classroom and uncover some important principles for creating classrooms that unleash student curiosity. You'll also receive the first of many tools this book offers to provide you with a tool kit of powerful and practical strategies for building a curious school.

Part III is based on the simple idea that if we want students to experience curiosity, we must also let *teachers* experience curiosity and the joy of discovery in their own professional learning. It provides important questions for leaders to ask as well as tools for creating school cultures that foster curiosity among students and adults.

Part IV shows how a complex form of curiosity—*interpersonal* curiosity—supports social-emotional learning, including greater compassion, better relationships, and stronger social bonds. It provides tools for helping students connect with one another and develop greater curiosity about other people's experiences and perspectives.

The last stop in our journey, Part V, describes what is arguably the most important correlate of curiosity: its link to well-being and happiness, often because curiosity can be a powerful consort to help students navigate emotional crises. We'll discover together how reflective curiosity can help students reexamine their own negative thoughts and develop personal formulas for happiness. As with the previous sections, it offers tools for helping students use curiosity to support their well-being.

Certainly, this isn't the first or only book written about curiosity. A plethora of researchers, academics, and journalists have crafted well-written books that offer important, compelling insights about curiosity. However, many of these books are written for a broad audience and thus offer few specific connections to classrooms and schools. This book, on the other hand, is **written for you and your professional learning community,** helping you learn together about the power of curiosity for students and providing you with practical strategies and tools to unleash curiosity in classrooms. This book is also unique in that it **aims to help entire school teams unleash curiosity across your whole school,** so all students can benefit from curiosity.

Perhaps, most importantly, this book draws upon McREL's deep knowledge of evidence-based practices of educators and, in so doing, **integrates brain-based research on the power of curiosity with research on effective schools and instruction** to help you and your colleagues create positive school cultures and classrooms that support deep, joyful learning. It also builds on an earlier McREL book, *Out of Curiosity*, by incorporating more practical tools and guidance for educators and a deeper discussion of the connections between curiosity and social-emotional learning.

Ultimately, while the book aims to be both interesting and practical, it aims to do something larger—something that goes beyond just tweaking lessons to make them a bit more interesting or adorning school hallways with inspirational posters about curiosity. It aims to help you put words and ideas to that nagging feeling you've had that something has gone wrong with our approach to teaching and learning. It aims to help all of us start a movement—coming as educators and school communities to push back against the forces that for too long have quashed our students' curiosity and joy of learning, so together, we can help students (and teachers) experience the joy of curiosity-fueled learning.

ACKNOWLEDGMENTS

Writing a book can be a lonely task, but it's never a solo endeavor. So, I'd like to thank many colleagues who have helped to shape this book in its winding journey over the past few years, starting with a team of dedicated colleagues at McREL—including Roger Fiedler and Eric Hubler, who lent their wizardry with words to early drafts of this manuscript, and Kris Rouleau and Ron Miletta, whose insightful feedback honed and sharpened the finished product.

I also owe a debt of gratitude to Fred Ende, Pete Hall, Duane "D.T." Magee, Kim Marshall, Harvey Silver, and Randy Ziegenfuss for reviewing earlier copies of this book, and to Wayne Craig and David Hopkins on whose shoulders and work in Melbourne, Australia I stood upon to write this book.

I'd also like to thank the talented crew at Corwin, including Arnis Burvikovs for believing in this book, Ariel Curry for taking it to the next level with her editorial guidance, Desirée Bartlett for supporting production of the final manuscript, Sharon Pendergast for getting it into readers' hands, and Eliza Erickson for just making things happen. In addition, a big thanks to Mike Soules for his patience and persistence in turning a someday possibility into reality.

Finally, to my daughters Sophie, Emma, and Molly, I can't wait to see the places you'll go with your intellectual, interpersonal, and spiritual curiosity. And to my wife, Kristi, thanks for chasing horizons with me and sharing (and tolerating) my many curiosities.

To all of you, thanks for making this book happen. I hope your lives are forever teeming with curiosity.

ABOUT THE AUTHOR

Bryan Goodwin is president and CEO of McREL International. For 20-plus years at McREL, he has translated research into practice, scanning the world for new insights and best practices on teaching and leading and helping educators everywhere adapt them to address their own challenges. A frequent conference presenter, he is the author of *Simply Better: Doing What Matters Most to Change the Odds for Student Success* and coauthor of *Curiosity Works: A Guidebook for Moving Your School From Improvement to Innovation*; *Unstuck: How Curiosity, Peer Coaching, and Teaming Can Change Your School*; *Balanced Leadership for Powerful Learning: Tools for Achieving Success in Your School*; and *The 12 Touchstones of Good Teaching: A Checklist for Staying Focused Every Day*. He also writes for ASCD's *Educational Leadership* magazine. Before joining McREL in 1998, Goodwin was a college instructor, a high school teacher, and business journalist.

PROLOGUE

A Cure for What Ails Us

The human brain had a vast memory storage. It made us curious and very creative. Those were the characteristics that gave us an advantage—curiosity, creativity and memory.

—David Suzuki

In the mid-1980s, Gary Swan and Dorit Carmelli (1996), researchers at SRI International, rounded up more than 1,000 men who had previously participated in a three-decade study of their health behavior and outcomes to ask them an unusual series of questions. By now, the men were all around 70 years old with plenty known about their medical histories: their blood pressure and cholesterol levels, frequency of drinking and smoking, whether they had fought cancer or heart disease, their education levels, cognitive abilities, and general mental health. Following a hunch that a subtle yet powerful dimension of personality might be a critical, hidden driver of their health outcomes, the researchers asked the men—and, for good measure, their wives—to respond to a 10-question survey . . . and then sat patiently on the answers for five years.

When they reconnected with the couples in 1991, they found that among the 2,000-plus people originally surveyed, 126 men and 78 women had passed away. That simple fact created a comparison group of survivors and nonsurvivors and invited a captivating question: Was there anything in the men's medical histories (no similar medical histories were available for the women) or in how they had answered those 10 simple questions five years earlier that might have predicted their shorter lifespans?

As it turns out, the answer was yes. How both men and women answered those questions revealed a subtle, yet powerful, facet of their personalities, which in turn appeared to predict their longevity.

The survivors demonstrated higher levels of a single, key personality trait than those who had died. In fact, for the men, only age and cancer seemed to be more predictive of their mortality. In other words, a personality trait appeared to be more strongly tied to their mortality than their cholesterol levels, smoking, education levels, and mental health. For both men and women, in fact, scoring one standard deviation above the mean (or at the 84th percentile) on the survey reduced their risk of dying five years later by about 30 percent.

So what was it? What personality trait helped these study participants live longer?

You'll find the answer on the following page.

Well done. You turned the page.

In a way, the simple action you just took reflects what the survivors in Swan and Carmelli's study were more capable of doing than nonsurvivors—demonstrating curiosity. The short personality test had asked the senior citizens to rate themselves on a scale of 1 to 4 on statements like these: "I feel like exploring my environment," "I feel stimulated," and "I feel eager."

At first, Swan and Carmelli were at a bit of a loss to explain exactly why such a strong link between curiosity and longevity would exist. One possibility, they surmised, might be that fading levels of curiosity are a canary in the coal mine, warning of the onset of Alzheimer's or other mental deterioration. Yet another possibility was that as people age they often face health and mobility challenges, so curiosity might predict whether they approach such challenges as solvable problems or succumb to despair and decreased interpersonal interactions, hastening their demise. All Swan and Carmelli could say for sure was that more curious seniors were more likely to be alive five years later.

CONFRONTING OUR CONTRADICTIONS ABOUT CURIOSITY

Despite this and many other powerful benefits of curiosity, we humans tend to have mixed views about it, both as individuals and as a society. Consider all the stories and inherited wisdom we've absorbed since our youth that paint curiosity as lurid fascination and temptation. In the Bible and Greek mythology, curiosity prompts Eve and Pandora, respectively, to unleash evil upon the world. Folk wisdom warns us about "curiosity killing the cat." And not so long ago, Eleanor Roosevelt found herself forced to defend her intellectual curiosity, which her critics groused was unbecoming of a First Lady. Even modern Internet searchers seem to harbor caution about curiosity: Type the words *is curiosity* into Google's search engine, and it autofills with the words *a sin*.

Certainly, at times, our need for intellectual closure and getting to the bottom of something, even if it means extracting lurid details, can reflect morbid curiosity, as researchers discovered when they sat students down at a table and told them to be careful with a pile of ballpoint pens left over from a previous experiment because some were electrified and would shock them if touched. As it turns out, like Pandora peering into her infamous box, the students couldn't resist the "shock value" (pun intended) of touching the pens (Hsee & Ruan, 2016). Thus, this little experiment appeared to demonstrate that curiosity may sometimes lead us to indulge in counterproductive or self-destructive urges.

COULD CURIOSITY BE A CURE FOR WHAT AILS US?

Nonetheless, as you'll discover in the chapters ahead, curiosity takes many forms. In its various incarnations, it has been shown to have far more positive consequences than negative ones, including the following:

- Priming the pump for learning. The more curious we are, the more we learn and recall later about our learning. Moreover, curiosity is more strongly linked to student success than IQ or persistence (Shah et al., 2018); however, the longer students stay in school, they less curious they become.

- Creating better leaders and more engaged school cultures. With 70 percent of employees—and teachers, for that matter—disengaged at work, school and district leaders should pay attention to this fact: Employee curiosity and engagement are strongly linked. Similarly, leaders' curiosity and their effectiveness are also linked, as well as the presence of curiosity in organizations and the success of those organizations.

- Supporting better relationships. When we're curious about others, we develop stronger relationships with them. However, interpersonal curiosity appears to be in dwindling supply, given the worrisome decline in college students' reported levels of empathy since the 1960s and an especially steep drop since 2000.

- Making our students' lives more fulfilling. On days when we feel curious, we also experience greater personal satisfaction; in short, people (and students) who report greater curiosity also report greater levels of happiness and life fulfillment.

What may be most enticing about curiosity is that it's not something we must learn or a skill to be developed. Rather, we're born curious. Yes, some people are more naturally curious than others. Yet as we'll see in this book, curiosity is hardwired in all of us. No one needs to teach us how to be curious.

That's the good news. Here's the bad news.

As we'll also see throughout this book, our childlike curiosity often wanes as we grow older and the longer students stay in school. As any parent knows, toddlers ask lots of questions, almost incessantly. Yet research shows that by the time kids reach school age, their questions come fewer and farther between; whereas toddlers ask up to 100 questions per day, middle schoolers' daily questions dwindle to nearly nil (Bronson & Merryman, 2010). In short, it appears that as we grow older and are subjected to formal schooling, we seem to run out of curiosity.

COME BACK, CURIOSITY . . .

Why should that be? Why should something as essential to what it means to be human beings start to fade when students enter our schools? Could it be that they simply acquire more information about their environment and thus have fewer questions about it? Or could it be that something in their environment tells them to stop asking so many questions and get back to their schoolwork? Or could it be that we put them on a need-to-know basis, telling them to accept the world around them as it is, no longer experiencing the joy of discovery?

To answer these questions, we'll look more deeply at what happens to kids' curiosity when they enter school—a place that, ostensibly at least, ought to be designed to unleash it. We'll also examine what happens to people (of all ages) when we're curious—and when we're not.

Knowing that curiosity leads to better learning, better organizations, and better lives might lead us to ask a larger question: What would it look like to unleash the deep kind of curiosity that lies at the heart of discovery, science, and enlightenment and serves as the lifeblood of democracy—across not just our schools, but an entire society? That is, what would it look like if we were to arrange more of our classrooms, schools, daily lives, and interactions with one another to do more things out of curiosity?

The purpose of this book is to focus our attention on the many (and often subtle) ways in which we seem to quash curiosity and what that means for our kids, our schools, our society, and happiness as human beings. More important, though, we'll explore how together we can restore curiosity in everything we do, making our classrooms and schools better, preparing our students to lead more fulfilling lives, and in so doing, creating a better society for us and them.

LET'S GET CURIOUS

While this book will offer some practical ways to instill curiosity in our classrooms, relationships, and organizations, it's not designed to be a how-to guide or step-by-step manual for creating more curious schools overnight (*Curiosity for Dummies*, if you will). Such a book would be counterproductive because, as we'll see, curiosity doesn't always serve an obvious purpose. Nor does it follow a straight line. Indeed, it's often only when we allow ourselves and our students to engage in some childlike wonder and to engage in a bit of intellectual wandering that we arrive at deeper meaning, richer learning, and greater success.

Thus, this book is intended to pique your curiosity (and your colleagues' curiosity if you're reading it as part of a book study) and provide you with a deeper appreciation for how so many aspects of our classrooms, schools, lives, and society are better when curiosity is present.

So if you're curious, let's start wondering and wandering.

PART I

GETTING CURIOUS ABOUT CURIOSITY

Research is formalized curiosity.

—Zora Neale Hurston

WHAT IS THIS
FUNNY LITTLE THING
CALLED CURIOSITY?

"Why is the grass green?"

"How come we can see the moon in the day?"

"Where did the dinosaurs go?"

Anyone who's been around a young child for very long knows the barrage of questions they ask, from the mundane ("What's the difference between a burrito and an enchilada?") to the profound ("Why do people die?") to the uncomfortable ("Where do babies come from?").

Sometimes, their questions challenge us, testing the limits of our own knowledge.

Shortly before bedtime one evening a few years ago, my daughter, Molly, who was seven at the time, suddenly became engrossed in the inner workings of the fluorescent lightbulbs in her ceiling lamp. "Why are the curlicue lights better?" she asked.

I suspected her question was a bedtime-stalling tactic but felt compelled to answer. "They use less electricity," I said.

However, my answer didn't satisfy her curiosity; she wanted to know *why* they use less electricity.

"They're not as hot, so they turn more electricity into light," I replied.

Still, she was curious: "Why don't they get as hot?"

I was fast approaching the limits of my knowledge of interior illumination, so I offered a vague explanation about lighting gas inside the tube instead of a filament, punctuated with a quip about it being time to turn off the lights and go to sleep.

The spontaneity and doggedness of her questions, though, made me curious. Where had her curiosity come from? After all, I'd done nothing to encourage it; her questions had emerged from the inner workings of her mind. And apart from achieving a delay in bedtime of a few seconds, her inquisitiveness didn't serve any purpose beyond the desire to learn for the sake of learning. In that regard, her curiosity seemed almost . . . well, sublime—a reflection of what truly makes us human—an innate desire to seek knowledge, truth, and meaning.

But I'm getting ahead of myself.

A STRANGE PHENOMENON

One of the first things we might wonder about curiosity is, simply, what the heck is it? And what causes it? We've all experienced the weirdness of curiosity—how it flashes in our minds like a bolt out of the blue, a sudden jolt or seemingly invisible hand tugging at the sleeves of our intellect and piquing our imagination.

At times, curiosity can be an irrational drive—a quest for information with little or no material benefit. Consider, for example, supermarket tabloids grabbing our interest in the lives of Hollywood stars. Even more strangely, perhaps, while this sort of curiosity can be a powerful impulse, it's often ephemeral; once through the checkout aisle, we rarely give another thought to those tabloid headlines.

For some, curiosity can manifest itself as a sort of thrill-seeking impulse. We can become curious, for example, about skydiving, riding a motorcycle, or jumping off a cliff into the ocean. Or maybe we're drawn to milder (and less risky) thrills, like learning to salsa dance, talking to a new neighbor at a party, or visiting Bhutan. Sometimes, we act on those impulses, and sometimes, we don't. Soon thereafter, the impulse often fades.

At the same time, we've all probably experienced another kind of less fleeting and more intellectual curiosity, something that drives us to keep searching for an answer, following one link after another on the Internet or filling our personal library with books on a particular topic that holds our fascination. In these cases, an initial spark of interest—often, we may even forget when or where it began—becomes a lifelong intellectual pursuit. This brand of deeper, more profound curiosity often lies at the heart of invention, science, and entrepreneurship—think of Thomas Edison and his team experimenting with hundreds of different metals before finally identifying tungsten as the best material for lightbulb filaments, or Jane Goodall spending months in the rain forest, patiently observing bands of gorillas. It's quite likely, in fact, that we owe most conveniences of modernity and scientific insights about our world to someone else's indefatigable curiosity.

A TWO-SIDED COIN

For these reasons, curiosity has long presented something of a puzzle to researchers. Over the past few decades of study and debate, psychologists have come up with a handful of different definitions, terms, and frameworks for curiosity, which generally fall into two main categories.

First, there's a spontaneous and ephemeral kind of curiosity, which over the years has been called *diversive* (Loewenstein, 1994) or *exploratory* (Engel, 2015a) curiosity. This kind of curiosity is typically triggered by external stimuli—something catches our fancy, providing us with an initial (and often impulsive) spark to explore our environment, an idea, or topic. When we experience this kind of curiosity, we may appear, in the words of curiosity researcher Susan Engel, to be "inquisitive and interested." However, an overabundance of this kind of curiosity can cause a person to appear easily "distractible." Teachers and parents might even grow concerned that their students or children are using curiosity to "distract others and prevent focus" (Engel, 2015a).

This fleeting kind of curiosity does not always serve a purpose. For example, we may wonder about a song lyric (are the Beach Boys really singing about "frying poultry in the sand"?) and go online for clarification (oh, "*by a palm tree* in the sand"). At this point, though, our initial curiosity, having led us to a website of misheard lyrics, could take us down a series of rabbit holes of other misheard lyrics. Thirty minutes or more may pass before we look at the clock and realize we've consumed valuable time following our curiosity and not really accomplishing anything.

All of this, of course, is far different from the kind of sustained curiosity that leads to inventing lightbulbs, developing a polio vaccine, or putting a man on the moon. This latter kind of curiosity entails sustained pursuit of challenging goals—a continued quest for knowledge even when the goal seems elusive. We tend to admire this sort of curiosity, while harboring mild disdain for the other. This fact may explain some of our ambivalence about curiosity. We've all experienced that in one form, curiosity can be a vice, and in another form, a virtue.

Curiosity researchers call this deeper and more sustained kind of curiosity *specific* or *informational* curiosity (Engel, 2015a; Loewenstein, 1994). As the more focused and self-directed cousin of diversive curiosity, it reflects the need "to find ever more information on a particular topic" (Engel, 2015a). Instead of flitting from one topic to the next, this second type of curiosity drives us to delve deeply into something and get smarter about it. It's often associated with inner drive to learn, stick-to-itiveness, and relentless pursuit of knowledge just beyond our reach.

In sum, we might think of diversive curiosity as those fleeting impulses to learn that we experience while looking at tabloids in the supermarket checkout aisle or overhearing a juicy conversation in the booth next to us at a restaurant. Specific or informational curiosity, on the other hand, is the more admirable or noble drive to understand something deeply, to experiment doggedly, and to master complex knowledge.

That said, we shouldn't regard one kind of curiosity as exclusively *good* and the other exclusively *bad*. Indeed, most people, according to researchers, display both kinds, albeit in differing levels of balance.

Moreover, these two kinds of curiosity can work hand-in-hand. All experts began as novices. First, they had to become interested in the topic, explore it a bit more, and eventually become engrossed in it. To pursue knowledge in depth, we need a spark of interest in the topic. Our natural human tendency, though, is to become less interested in something as we become more familiar with it.

Thus, we need new sparks of interest to stay engaged in our pursuits: To remain curious about something long enough to explore it deeply, we must continually find new wrinkles or surprises in it that make it feel new again, compelling us to dig deeper.

WHAT SPARKS CURIOSITY?

At this point, we might wonder (or, ahem, feel *curious* about), what exactly creates curiosity? Where does curiosity come from—how does it spring forth from our consciousness and spark our seemingly spontaneous impulses to learn? Over the years, numerous experiments have teased out the conditions that arouse curiosity—many of which we can easily reproduce in a classroom, faculty meeting, conversation with a friend, or presentation to a large audience. Here's a starter list drawn from a synthesis conducted by one of the preeminent names in the field of curiosity research, George Loewenstein (1994).

- Manageable knowledge gaps. Fundamentally, we become curious when we experience a gap in our knowledge. That's why we're suckers for incomplete sequences (e.g., 1, 2, 3, 5, 8 . . . what comes next?) and unfinished narratives (e.g., a cliffhanger prior to a commercial break). Riddles and puzzles also fit into this category, especially when we have a "reference point" with them (Loewenstein, 1994, p. 87). Studies have shown, in fact, that we tend to become more interested in a topic when we (a) know something about it and (b) feel our knowledge gap closing (Kang et al., 2009). This explains why it's much harder to put down a mystery novel five pages from the ending than five pages from the beginning.

- Guessing and receiving feedback. To become curious about something, we must also become aware of our knowledge gap—that is, we must realize we don't know something about a topic of interest to us. Studies have found, for example, that when we receive "accuracy feedback"—making a guess and learning we have guessed wrong—we want to learn the correct answer. In his own research, Loewenstein (1994) found people became more interested to learn the easternmost state in the US after they made a guess (and received accuracy feedback) about the westernmost state in the nation. (If you're curious, the answer is Alaska for both questions, as a handful of Aleutian Islands lie in the Eastern Hemisphere.)

- Incongruities. We also become curious when we encounter something that doesn't fit our expectations. Consider, for example, the spark of curiosity you likely feel when you learn (or learned) that winds blowing down from mountaintops into valleys below can sometimes be warm, not cold, or that offering fewer flavor choices of jams in a supermarket display encourages people to buy more jars of jam. In both cases, you may find yourself wondering, why is that?

- Controversy. Researchers have also found that controversy begets curiosity. In a now-famous experiment, researchers randomly assigned fifth- and sixth-grade students to work in groups. One group was instructed to engage in cooperative learning about a topic (for example, strip mining or designating wolves as an endangered species); the other was encouraged to focus on controversy in the topic. Students in the controversy condition demonstrated more interest in the topic, sought more information on it, and were more likely to give up a recess period to watch a film about it (Lowry & Johnson, 1981).

- Someone knows something we don't. We might call this the "I-have-a-secret" phenomenon. For example, a friend telling us she or he has bought a great present for us but won't tell us what it is until our birthday or hearing someone sitting next to us chuckle while reading a magazine article are both apt to make us curious.

What all of this suggests is that there are a number of ways our external environment can arouse our curiosity.

Yet we might wonder about people who seem to be perpetually curious. They don't simply respond to stimuli but rather seem to spark their own curiosity. They're always asking questions, reading books, wondering about ideas, exploring new places, and meeting new people. They have a knack for looking at something that others find bland or boring and finding something interesting about it. That knack seems like a different, deeper, and more internalized form of curiosity than the fleeting variety triggered by conditions in our external environment.

It is.

These conditions (we might even say gimmicks) for creating curiosity are all fairly task-specific and reflect what researchers call *state curiosity*. Such ephemeral forms of curiosity are a far cry, of course, from the form of curiosity that comes to mind when we think of a Jane Goodall, Albert Einstein, or Marie Curie—people with insatiable intellectual appetites who keep asking questions. They're not just curious from time to time, but always curious. This kind of deeper, more internalized curiosity reflects what many researchers call *trait curiosity*.

BECOMING CURIOUS PEOPLE

It's trait curiosity that's most often linked to positive outcomes in school, the workplace, and life itself. Trait curiosity gives us a fire inside to keep learning, even in the face of challenges. People with high levels of trait curiosity are curious as people. We might think of it as the difference between an *-ing* or *-er* ending on verbs. It's one thing to say we're writing, swimming, singing, or inquiring, and something different to call ourselves writers, swimmers, singers, or inquirers. So, too, it's one thing to say I *feel* curious, and something different to say I *am* curious.

As we'll see throughout this book, it's this latter form of trait curiosity that's typically linked to better academic performance, relationships, job performance, and the like. New studies are finding, though, that trait curiosity itself is not a single, monolithic characteristic but rather takes different forms, including "joyous exploration" (seeking novel stimuli), "social curiosity" (seeking to understand others), "stress tolerance" (embracing ambiguity), "deprivation sensitivity" (focused problem-solving), and "thrill seeking" (being open to novel and even risky experiences; Kashdan et al., 2018). Although researchers continue to study (and debate) how to define and categorize curiosity, for our purposes it may be helpful to picture curiosity as sorting out something like this:

Figure 1.1   Visualizing Curiosity

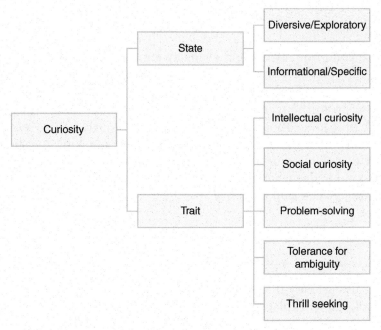

Creating these two big "buckets" of state and trait curiosity prompts a nature-versus-nurture question—specifically, is trait curiosity something innate, a personality characteristic (as the label might suggest), and accordingly, a product of nature? In other words, are some people naturally predisposed to be more curious than others? Or, instead, is trait curiosity more of a discipline—something akin to a talent, like singing, that has elements of nature (some people are gifted with better vocal cords than others), but nevertheless, can be nurtured and developed?

The answer to this question has profound implications. If curiosity is in our stars (or genes), that would mean some people are born to be more curious—and thus destined to lead happier, more successful, and longer lives—while the rest of humanity is fated to toil away in a humdrum, incurious existence. If, on the other hand, curiosity is a trait we can *develop*, we ought to contemplate another question altogether, especially in light of the wide variance researchers observe in people's reported levels of curiosity: Why do so many people seem to lose their curiosity or struggle to rekindle it?

As we'll discover in the next chapter, our search for an answer to this question of whether curiosity is borne more out of nature or nurture will take us on a winding road with a few surprises lurking around each corner.

ARE WE NATURALLY CURIOUS?

In his book *Dad Is Fat*, comedian Jim Gaffigan (2013), a father of five children, recounts the incessant questions young children ask:

> They learn to speak. And the questions commence. Anyone with kids knows about questions. "Daddy, what are you doing? Daddy, why are you doing that? Daddy, how long are you going to be doing that? Daddy, why are you putting on headphones and having a beer for breakfast?" (pp. 117–118)

The humor in Gaffigan's experiences reflects, of course, what anyone who's been around children for much time at all knows: They're full of questions. They're curious, incessantly (and at times annoyingly) so.

That's because, as cognitive psychologist John Medina (2008) has observed, human beings are hardwired to be curious. Our natural propensity for curiosity, in fact, likely contributed to our ability to survive and thrive as a species—mastering fire, horticulture, shelter construction, hunting, and oceanic navigation—the list goes on and on. Human infants, Medina observes, are natural-born scientists; they are constantly exploring their environments, grasping for objects, and putting them in their mouths. Preschoolers in laboratory experiments, for example, show more interest in toys that work in unexplained ways than those they've already figured out (Schulz & Bonawitz, 2007).

Nonetheless, as with most phenomena, researchers have observed variations in exactly how much curiosity infants and toddlers demonstrate. Some appear to be more prone to curiosity, demonstrating greater levels of what's called "stimulation seeking" (e.g., investigating new objects in their environments) than others. A longitudinal study of 1,795 children, for example, found that as three-year-olds, they demonstrated considerable variance in stimulation seeking; eight years later, those who had demonstrated greater stimulation seeking as toddlers scored 12 points higher on IQ tests than their lower stimulation-seeking peers (Raine et al., 2002).

On one hand, finding significant differences in curiosity among young children might suggest it's an ingrained genetic response—more a product of nature than nurture. Yet as a growing body of research shows, early childhood experiences have a tremendous impact on all manner of life outcomes—from kindergarten readiness to school performance to mental health and well-being. So what is it? Is curiosity a matter of nature . . . or nurture?

IS CURIOSITY IN OUR DNA?

Let's start with this thought experiment: Imagine two twins separated at birth. One goes to a home with highly curious parents who lavish their children with books to read, trips to local museums, opportunities to explore the natural world, and riveting conversations about literature, science, philosophy, and current events. The other goes to a home where ennui hangs in the air; bookshelves are empty, family conversations vapid, and opportunities for children to engage their curiosity few. Would both twins emerge from these environments equally curious?

If curiosity were purely a matter of genetics, the answer would be yes. If hard-wired to be curious, we'd expect the twins to display an equally strong desire to explore, learn, and get to the bottom of questions, regardless of the stimulation or tedium of their home environments (or conversely, the same world-weary boredom if they lacked the curiosity "gene").

As it turns out, researchers have actually managed to, in effect, replicate our thought experiment by locating and studying hundreds of pairs of twins separated at birth—people who share the same *nature*, yet experience different *nurture*. In one such study, a team of researchers (Steger et al., 2007) analyzed how 336 middle-aged twins (both identical and fraternal) separated at birth responded to a survey of 24 positive character traits, one of which included curiosity. Despite being raised in different homes with no connection to one another, the twins often demonstrated remarkably similar personality traits—sometimes uncannily so.

For example, one of the most famous pairs in the sample, the so-called "Jim Twins," Jim Lewis and Jim Springer, had been separated at four weeks old and not reunited until they were 39. Despite their time apart, they had both given their dogs the same name (Toy), married first and *second* wives with the same names (Linda and Betty, respectively), named their sons James Alan (though one was spelled James Allan), smoked the same cigarettes (Salem), drank the same beer (Miller Lite), drove the same kind of car (a light-blue Chevy), vacationed in the same three-block stretch of a Florida beach without ever meeting, worked as part-time sheriffs, and chewed their fingernails (Segal, 2000).

Given such striking similarities among twins, we might expect to see them share remarkably similar levels of curiosity as well, especially if curiosity were purely genetic, like eye or hair color. Yet that's not quite what researchers found when they compared the differences in responses to questions regarding curiosity among identical twins (who share 100 percent of the same genes), fraternal twins (who share 50% of the same genes), and the general population. Yes, there were some similarities, but hardly an exact match—akin to vacationing in the same state, but not the same stretch of beach. Overall, the research team determined that the percentage of variance in curiosity that could be chalked up to heredity was about 21 percent. Basically, our genes appear to *influence*, but not dictate, how curious we are in life.

Recent studies have, in fact, isolated some genetic differences that may explain why some people are more predisposed to curiosity than others, including genes related to novelty seeking and impulsivity (Munafò et al., 2008) or viewing new experiences as threatening or exciting (Grazioplene et al., 2013). Nonetheless, curiosity is not a binary trait—something we either have or do not have. Rather, it's a matter of degree. Some people are mildly curious, others moderately curious, and others immensely curious. Yes, nature plays a supporting role in our curiosity, but, as we'll see, nurture appears to play the starring role.

Indeed, studies going back decades have concluded that from an early age, children's home environments influence how comfortable they feel exploring their worlds (Endsley et al., 1979). Over the course of hundreds of cross-cultural experiments in the late 50s and 60s, Mary Ainsworth, for example, found that infants who were more "securely attached" to their mothers—who could use them as a "secure base" from which to venture out and explore their environments—were more apt to demonstrate curiosity and problem-solving as toddlers (Ainsworth et al., 2015). These and later studies led researchers to conclude that children tend to be more curious when they're exposed to parenting styles that are *authoritative* (clear, consistent rules with warmth and support) as opposed to parenting styles that are *authoritarian* (demanding without warmth—"do as I say or else"), *permissive* (warm but not demanding), or *uninvolved* (neither warm nor demanding; Rivers et al., 2012).

Early on, infants' and toddlers' interactions with their environments and parents create feedback loops that can instill or inhibit curiosity, making them view their worlds as either desirable or dangerous (Shulman, 2002). By about 21 months of age, these differences begin to solidify into observable patterns of behavior—from inhibition to openness to new situations, places, and people—that persist as children reach school age (Kagan et al., 1989).

So does that mean genetics, home environments, and early childhood experiences conspire to set our "curiosity dials" at a permanent level for the rest of our lives?

Not exactly.

It's true that on one hand, people's curiosity dials may be set at any early age. Moreover, most adults' levels of curiosity stay pretty much the same—or even decline—over the course of their lifetimes (Giambra et al., 1992). Yet when it comes to curiosity, neither genetics nor early experiences need to be a fait accompli. Indeed, as we'll see, many interesting experiments suggest that regardless of where kids' curiosity dials may be set, relatively simple (and often subtle) tweaks to their environments can reignite their curiosity—tapping into their natural (albeit sometimes latent) desire to explore their worlds, find pleasure in new experiences, and experience the joy of discovery.

Let's start here: Over the years, many studies have shown that environmental conditions—including how teachers and other adults interact with children—significantly influence their openness to exploration. For example, a study of 40 preschool children found that children were more apt to explore their surroundings in the presence of a friendly, supportive adult than in the company of an aloof, critical one (Moore & Bulbulian, 1976). In another study, adults were directed to interact with students in three different ways:

- Answering students' questions with only brief, direct responses to encourage their independence

- Demonstrating active interest in students' curiosity by encouraging their inquisitiveness with smiles and eye contact and attentiveness

- Focusing their interest by asking pointed follow-up questions to encourage further exploration of topics

The latter two conditions—demonstrating active interest in students' curiosity and focusing their interests—were found to support more exploratory behavior, especially among children whose teachers or parents had initially identified them as having low levels of curiosity (Henderson & Moore, 1980). This last point is important because it suggests that kids' curiosity is not solely a function of parenting or maternal bonds; even brief interaction with other supportive adults can help kids find and unleash curiosity within themselves.

In a more recent study, Tessa van Schijndel and her colleagues (2010) sent preschool children into a children's museum under three different conditions: (1) an adult accompanying the children, offering minimal interaction beyond some words of encouragement (e.g., "This is a nice game, isn't it?"); (2) an adult providing thought-provoking questions (e.g., asking at an exhibit where children rolled cylinders down tracks with different surfaces, "Does the one on this track go as fast as the one on that track? How is that possible?"); and (3) an adult teaching the science of exhibits directly to the children (e.g., "The one on this track goes faster because this track is smoother than the other track"). As it turns out, the second condition—asking thought-provoking questions to guide exploration—proved most beneficial, while assuming the role of teacher backfired; children lost interest in the exhibits when adults came right out and explained them, seemingly quashing the joy of discovery (van Schijndel et al., 2010).

ARE SOME CLASSROOMS MORE CURIOUS THAN OTHERS?

Along similar lines, through a series of classroom experiments, Susan Engel, a preeminent researcher of children's curiosity, showed that regardless of where students' "curiosity dials" may have been set through nature or nurture, their teachers can readily turn those dials up (or down). Engel and her student, Hilary Hackmann, placed a "curiosity box"—a wooden cabinet with 18 drawers containing novelty items—in several different elementary school classrooms, accompanied with a sign that read, "Okay to touch." Then, they quietly observed the classrooms to see how students would interact with it, how many students would approach the box, and how many drawers they'd open to experience the joy of discovering the tiny surprises inside.

If curiosity were simply a matter of genetics or parental programming, we might expect to see every classroom reflect a similar bell curve of variable interactions with the box: Some children would fully engage with it, opening every drawer; some might be mildly interested in it, trying a few drawers; and others would ignore it altogether.

Yet that's not what Engel and Hackmann found. Instead, they observed variability among classrooms—that is, in some classrooms nearly every student actively engaged with the box. Upon seeing it in the back of their classrooms, they would say things like, "What is that?" "Whoa, where did that come from?" and "It says OK to touch, so I'm going to touch it." Meanwhile, in other classrooms students scarcely laid a finger on the mysterious box in the back of the room. Why was that? As it turns out, the critical link was "how much the teacher smiled and talked in an encouraging manner and the level of curiosity children in the room expressed" (Engel, 2015b, p. 77).

Engel and Hackmann, in fact, found a direct link between the number of smiles and encouraging words the teachers offered and students' exploration of the curiosity box. In classrooms where students explored the box, teachers would say things like, "What do you have there? Wow, I think you really like that thing. That's cool. Look at that." Meanwhile, in classrooms where students would ignore the box, teachers would say things like, "Rachel, turn your body around and do your work" (i.e., stop looking at the box), or "I saw some of you up there by the box, and you owe me Friday's English" (Engel, 2015b, p. 77).

A CURIOUS CHILDHOOD

Decades ago, Mildred Goertzel, a teacher of emotionally disturbed children, and her husband Victor Goertzel, a clinical psychologist, found themselves in the embarrassing position of not knowing what to do about their eldest of three sons, Ted, a smart child who was underachieving in school and having difficulty making friends (Goertzel, 2004). It was the late 1950s, and not much was known about gifted children like Ted—nor were there any support groups or websites from which to glean information. So Mildred went to the local library, and walking past the shelves of books on psychology and child development (she already knew plenty about both topics), she began looking for biographies of famous, gifted people who had made special contributions throughout history and who she hoped might serve as role models for her sons.

As she consumed the biographies of hundreds of luminaries, including Eleanor Roosevelt, Winston Churchill, Mahatma Gandhi, and Theodore Roosevelt, and shared them with her husband, they realized she had unearthed a treasure trove of information overlooked by most researchers. They decided to write a book together—not for academics and educators, but for parents like themselves who were struggling to raise gifted children. Over the next few decades, the Goertzels and their son Ted would scour biographies of hundreds of other highly accomplished people—including Neil Armstrong, Martin Luther King Jr., Steve Jobs, and Oprah Winfrey—and report their findings in several books that would identify some peculiar common themes among these people's childhood experiences (Goertzel et al., 2004).

The first thing to jump off the pages of these biographies was that the childhood homes of these distinguished individuals all reflected a love for learning and a persistent drive toward ambitious goals. That much perhaps was to be expected. What was less expected, though, was that many of these high achievers also spent considerable time out of school, exploring their environments. Fully four-fifths of them showed great promise in school, yet three-fifths of them expressed dissatisfaction with their school experiences, apparently gaining far more from their own academic exploration, which was often supported by tutoring from their parents or others.

In other words, the greatest achievers in history were often *unschooled* as much as they were schooled. Given what we now know about how schooling so often tends to quash curiosity and (as we'll see throughout this book) how powerful curiosity is for fueling lifelong success, it perhaps only stands to reason that the world's most influential people spent much of their childhoods learning independently—often with the aid of a mentor who let them explore their environments. It's an insight that bears repeating—great achievers had time to explore their environments. They were not forced to learn; rather, they had freedom of choice to find their own sparks of interest and fan them into flames of sustained interest.

Curiosity, as it turns out, cannot be forced. We cannot make students become curious; rather, we must lead them to it by creating environments and opportunities for curiosity to flourish.

What all of this suggests is that curiosity isn't taught or compelled but rather emerges like a sprouting plant when the conditions are right. In short, the environments we create for children—at home, in school, and elsewhere—can cause curiosity to grow or wilt. And, as we'll see later in this book, the same appears to be true for adults: The school cultures we create for ourselves can either summon or suppress our professional curiosity.

These insights might lead us to another question: What exactly is going on in our brains when we're curious? Why are spontaneous sparks of interest so essential to learning? Can we learn without being curious? Here, a whole new generation of neuroscience is enabling researchers to peer into our brains—often at the precise moment that sparks of curiosity occur—and in so doing, reveal the exact parts of our brains that fire in an explosion of chemicals when we're curious.

Through this modern science, we're finding that curiosity serves as a Sherpa of sorts for new knowledge, shouldering new ideas down a long and perilous journey to a final destination in our long-term memories. Sure, learning can happen without curiosity, but like a mountain climber without a guide, it's more apt to get lost along the way when curiosity is absent.

On top of that, as we'll see, satisfying our curiosity—closing those nagging gaps in our knowledge—floods our brains with "feel-good" chemicals, so much so that it seems entirely possible to develop an "addiction" to seeking and finding new knowledge. In other words, we can be addicted to exploration, discovery, and novelty.

And what exactly do we call these addicts? We call them curious, of course.

3

THIS IS YOUR BRAIN ON CURIOSITY

Imagine, for a moment, that you're working in an ice cream parlor that serves only two types of ice cream, chocolate or vanilla. To expedite service, you've been asked to predict customers' orders based solely on clues in their appearance. Your customers, as it turns out, are Mr. Potato Head dolls, and their physical features are limited to permutations of bow tie, mustache, glasses, and hat.

By this point, you've probably figured out you're playing a game—in this case, one created by a team of researchers in Massachusetts who want to find out what exactly happens in our brains during cliffhanger moments of suspense while we're awaiting a resolution to our curiosity (Aron et al., 2004). During the study, images of different "customers" (i.e., different versions of Mr. Potato Head) appear in front of your eyes for a few seconds, and you're asked to press one of two buttons, representing chocolate or vanilla, to make your prediction. Afterward, the screen goes dark for a few seconds (building suspense) before flashing an answer: Mr. Potato Head, holding either a chocolate or vanilla ice cream cone.

After repeated guesses and feedback, you start to get better at detecting the pattern and getting more right answers after those tantalizing moments of suspense. When you get the correct answer, you feel a buzz of elation in your brain, like the ding! ding! ding! of hitting a jackpot on a slot machine. Throughout the whole experiment, your brain has been connected to an imaging device that provides a fascinating insight to researchers conducting the study: During that brief moment when you learned you guessed the correct answer, your brain activated a reward center that released dopamine into your system.

Because dopamine provides the sensation of pleasure, it's also at the root of many habits and addictions—both bad and good—which means that the intellectual exercise of satisfying our curiosity is likely to be habit forming. When we feel curious, we want to satisfy our curiosity because we know that when we do, we'll experience a little moment of joy. As a result, we begin to crave it.

MAKING MEMORIES STICK

Brain science also reveals that, in addition to creating a positive craving, the more curiosity drives our learning, the more likely we are to recall what we've learned later. As researchers at the University of California, Davis, discovered in an unusual experiment (Gruber et al., 2014), simply being in a state of heightened curiosity makes us more susceptible to learning new knowledge—even information irrelevant to what sparked our initial curiosity.

Here's how the study worked. Initially, the researchers asked participants to review a list of trivia questions (What does the term *dinosaur* really mean? Who was president of the US when Uncle Sam first got a beard?) and indicate how likely they were to know the answer and how curious each question made them. In a second phase of the study, the participants reread the questions that were now divided into two sets—those that made them curious and those that did not. After each question, the study participants viewed an image of a person's face for 14 seconds before finally learning the answer to the trivia question—all while having their brains scanned by an imaging device.

A day later, the study participants returned to the lab, and the researchers quizzed them on not only the right answers to the questions but also the faces they had seen. As it turns out, the participants could better recall both the answers to questions for which they reported higher levels of curiosity as well as the irrelevant images of people's faces that had preceded answers to their questions. In short, curiosity seems to have primed their brains for learning and knowledge retention. Brain scans confirmed this: When participants reported being curious, their brains' dopamine-releasing reward centers were activated, followed by increased activity in the hippocampus, which is involved in the creation of memories.

CURIOUSER AND CURIOUSER

In light of the addictive nature of curiosity, it may create a phenomenon similar to what reading researchers call the Matthew effect, named for the passage in the Gospel of Matthew that refers to the rich getting richer and the poor getting poorer. Studies have shown that students who are more capable of reading find it more enjoyable, and thus read more and become even better (richer) readers, while poor readers tend to read less and thus become, in relative terms, even poorer readers (Stanovich, 1986).

Similarly, when it comes to curiosity, the curious may become curiouser, and the incurious may become less curious, or simply bored. Recall that curiosity is associated with dopamine spikes in our brains—the same chemical that gets released when we encounter any kind of novel event, be it seeing a new movie, hearing a funny joke, pleasing our taste buds, or experiencing our first kiss. However, we also know from brain research that novel events produce diminishing returns when it comes to dopamine. Thus, as we encounter the same stimuli over and over (a process known as habituation), our dopamine levels decrease—which explains why songs grow tiresome after too many hearings, jokes get old after too much repeating, eating the same thing for lunch every day loses its pleasure, and romance can fade months or years after that first kiss.

It also explains why, to remain curious about something (or someone), we need to continually ask new questions and make new discoveries—like discovering a new favorite musical artist, finding new recipes for lunchtime salads and sandwiches, or learning that our long-term romantic partner also likes piña coladas and getting caught in the rain (hat tip to Rupert Holmes).

The point here is that our brains are hardwired to seek new stimuli—the question is which stimuli will we use to fill that need? As we'll see in later chapters, curious people learn to satisfy their thirst for novelty through intellectual stimulation—for example, continually expanding the repertoire of songs they play on the guitar or developing deeper relationships with their romantic partners. The less curious, on the other hand, who haven't trained their brains to crave intellectual stimulation, may seek it through physical or chemical stimulation or self-destructive behaviors. Indeed, counselors often find that boredom lies at the heart of many drug addictions; teaching addicts to overcome boredom through more constructive novelty seeking is often the key to avoiding relapse (Heshmat, 2015).

THE CURIOUS NATURE OF CURIOSITY RESEARCH

A caveat: As we move beyond neuroscientific studies of the brain and dig deeper into research on curiosity, we'll plunge into what some view as the spongy center of a great deal of social science and psychology research: self-reported survey data and correlational findings. As with many measures of personality and thinking styles, researchers continue to debate the accuracy of curiosity scales, often because of their reliance on asking people to self-report personal preferences and/or their daily behaviors—which requires that their subjects provide honest and accurate answers.

Nonetheless, as we'll see throughout this book, these surveys do generate a wide array of results, which suggests people responding to them seem to do so honestly, revealing what would appear to be genuine differences in their dispositions and behavior. Researchers can thus compare these variances in self-reported curiosity with other data, like academic learning, job performance, and interpersonal relationships, and in so doing, arrive at some intriguing and often surprising findings.

At the same time, it's worth noting that as we dive into research on curiosity, we'll also encounter what can be a frustrating fluidity of terminology and concepts. Already, you may be wondering: Why are there two terms, *diversive* and *exploratory*, and not just one, to describe the same sort of curiosity? Candidly, one reason for this is likely the "publish-or-perish" reality of academia, in which researchers are more apt to make a name for themselves by creating their own frameworks and models than by latching onto someone else's concepts or replicating their studies. Another reason, though, is that we're talking about the complex inner workings of the human mind and even more complex relationships of people to their environments—things we cannot subject to the same sort of empirical research as, say, giving an experimental group a dose of medicine (i.e., a curiosity pill) and a control group a sugar-pill placebo. So we're left with researchers' earnest attempts to connect dots and make sense of best-available data and their resulting theories and frameworks.

In the end, curiosity may remain an abstract concept that we can never completely pin down, leaving us with insights that may feel like we're trying to make sense of the shadows on the wall in Plato's famous *Allegory of the Cave*—more a reflection of reality than a precise measure of it. Nonetheless, if we can accept the inherent squishiness of some of this research and keep our minds open to the metaphors, constructs, and theories that researchers use to encircle a complex and messy phenomenon, we can arrive together at some compelling insights about the nature of curiosity, which, in turn, can have some profound implications for our students and even our own happiness.

PART II

CURIOSITY IN CLASSROOMS

Kids are born curious about the world. What adults primarily do in the presence of kids is unwittingly thwart the curiosity of children.

—Neil deGrasse Tyson

QUASHING
CURIOSITY

One snowy morning not so long ago, I met my youngest daughter Molly, who was then in first grade (about the same time she quizzed me on fluorescent lighting), coming down the stairs on her way to breakfast while I was going upstairs to get ready for work.

"Is this a school day?" she asked.

With a snow falling outside in a spring snowstorm (common in Colorado, where we live), I figured she was hoping for a snow day. "Yes, you still have school today," I informed her, expecting her shoulders to slump dejectedly.

Instead, she pumped her fist and exclaimed, "Yes!"

As a parent, I was elated; my child was happy it *wasn't* a snow day. As it happens, Molly's excitement about going to school had bubbled straight out of her curiosity; the day before, her class had begun an overnight science experiment, and she couldn't wait to return to school to see what had happened.

While driving my other daughters to school that morning, I asked Emma, in middle school at the time, how she felt about going to school. "Sleepy, but excited," she said before listing a couple of interesting things in store for her, including an "invention convention" project she was busily preparing for a school fair. I asked my eldest daughter, Sophie, then in high school, if she shared Molly's excitement for school. "Yes, I'm super excited," she responded, but with wry teenage sarcasm. Eventually, she allowed that she was excited to be playing in a tennis meet that afternoon (providing the snow melted), having just joined the junior varsity team.

TURNING TALENT AND INTEREST INTO BOREDOM

As parents, we'd like to imagine that when we send our kids off to school, they'll be entering environments that challenge them to learn what they need to be successful in life, as well as spark their interest in learning. Yet the pattern I saw in my own daughters that morning reflects national trends—the longer students stay in school, the less intrinsic motivation they report in their core subjects. A Gallup Organization survey of some 500,000 students, for example, found that roughly 8 in 10 elementary students felt "engaged" in school—that is, attentive, curious, and optimistic about their learning—yet by high school, that number had plummeted to just 4 in 10 students feeling engaged (Busteed, 2013). And according to a longitudinal study of more than 100 students (called the Fullerton Study), while high schoolers remained interested in school overall, their engagement was bolstered largely by extracurriculars, which overshadow their waning interest in regular classes (Gottfried et al., 2001).

More than two decades ago, Mihaly Csikszentmihalyi (pronounced *cheek-sent-me-high*) and his colleagues discovered much the same phenomenon when they set out to determine why some teenagers nurture their talents and others do not (Csikszentmihalyi et al., 1993). In many ways, they set out to study what we might call the high school yearbook paradox. We probably all know people from school who everyone assumed would accomplish great things, voted "most likely" to succeed in sports, music, arts, business, or politics. Years later, though, we may have bumped into them on the street, caught up with them at a reunion, or found them on Facebook and been surprised to see they hadn't realized their early potential—they didn't move to Hollywood, become a sports star, or become a rocket scientist as everyone had assumed. Conversely, we've probably all had classmates who unexpectedly achieved some form of success or even stardom in their chosen fields; somehow, they took a dormant or nascent talent and doggedly cultivated it, surprising more than a few people along the way.

The question that Csikszentmihalyi and his colleagues sought to answer was this: What does it take for teenagers to nurture their talents and interests long enough to develop expertise?

For the study, they found 208 teenagers identified by teachers as having exceptional promise in art, music, mathematics, science, or athletics and set out to see how they spent their days and what they did, or did not do, to cultivate their talents. Using the technology of the day—pagers—they pinged students at random intervals throughout the day and asked them to record what they were doing and their level of engagement while doing it.

Specifically, they were curious whether the students' school experiences offered any periods of optimal motivation required to cultivate talents—a condition Csikszentmihalyi had earlier dubbed *flow*, or a sort of Cinderella-at-the-ball experience marked by "losing track of time and being unaware of fatigue and of everything else but the activity itself" (Csikszentmihalyi et al., p. 14).

The resulting in-depth portrait of the teenagers' lives offers a gloomy picture of high school life, which (if the Gallup study is any indication) likely hasn't changed much since then. While in class, most students reported high levels of concentration but low levels of interest, even in subjects in which they were highly skilled. In many classrooms, teachers seemed to leech joy from learning by not explaining its purpose or applying it to the outside world. As one talented yet disappointed math student noted, "Once you have the theorem down, it would help you to know how you could use it, instead of just strictly what it is. I think it makes it more interesting and easier to learn" (Csikszentmihalyi et al., p. 183).

BORED TO DEATH

Csikszentmihalyi and colleagues' (1993) observations are reflected in other studies as well, which have found that the longer children stay in school, the less curiosity they demonstrate or are encouraged to demonstrate. For example, in his studies of school-age children dating back to the 1960s, creativity researcher Paul Torrance found that while teachers said they viewed curiosity as important, they typically did not identify their best students as those who demonstrated curiosity (Torrance, 1963). Moreover, while 72 percent of elementary teachers said they valued students' unusual questions, only 42 percent of middle school educators said likewise (Torrance, 1965).

A study in the 1980s found a similar pattern of declining emphasis on student curiosity among classroom teachers. In second and third grades, fully 65 percent of teachers surveyed reported that they encouraged curiosity in their classrooms. Yet in fourth and fifth grades, that number had dropped to 41 percent of teachers (Engelhard, 1985). In a follow-up study of 298 students in third, fifth, and seventh grades enrolled in a predominantly white Catholic school in a working-class neighborhood and a predominantly black public school in the Midwestern US, researchers found the same pattern: In both settings, school-related curiosity decreased as children grew older (Engelhard & Monsaas, 1988).

Through her series of classroom observations, Susan Engel (2011), whom we met earlier with her "curiosity box" experiment, found kindergarten students displaying, on average, 2.36 episodes of curiosity over a two-hour period. By fifth grade, however, that number had dropped to 0.48 episodes in a two-hour period, which suggests that many children spend their entire school day "without asking even one question or engaging in one sequence of behavior aimed at finding out something new" (p. 633). And by the time students reach high school, surveys have found that nearly two-thirds of students (65 percent) report being bored in class on a daily basis, with just 2 percent reporting never feeling bored; the top two reasons they cite for being bored is that classroom material is uninteresting (82 percent) or not personally relevant to them (41 percent; Yazzie-Mintz, 2010).

NO TIME FOR CURIOSITY

Granted, high school boredom is hardly a new phenomenon; we probably all have some flashbacks of high school tedium and chuckle when we see Ben Stein's deadpan lecture in *Ferris Bueller's Day Off*. Yet when you think about it, that ought to strike us as odd. After all, our schools ought to be rife with curiosity, especially as students enter middle and high school where they can learn science that unravels the mysteries of the universe, experience great literature that provides deep insights into the human condition, and learn mathematics to solve complex, real-life problems.

But instead, many classrooms appear to be completely misaligned with what sparks curiosity. For example, video comparisons with other countries find that when it comes to mathematics instruction, American teachers commonly downgrade complex problems into simple tasks, turning intriguing and curiosity-evoking challenges—such as figuring out how to calculate the area of a triangle—into spoon-fed formulas (Stigler & Hiebert, 2004). American teachers seem to be in such a hurry to cut to the chase and give students the right answer that students experience little of the joy (or critical thinking) that comes from wrapping their minds around challenging problems and working out the answer.

In other words, many educators appear to be designing and delivering classroom lessons in a manner that runs counter to what we know about how curiosity is sparked and sustained. Or as cognitive scientist John Medina (2008) has observed, "If you wanted to create an education environment that was directly opposed to what the brain was good at doing, you probably would design something like a classroom" (p. 5).

Yet before we pile on teachers and blame them for creating humdrum classrooms, we might consider the observation attributed to various organizational theorists, including W. Edwards Deming, Don Berwick, and Paul Batalden: "Every system is perfectly designed to get the result that it does" (IHI, 2015). So if our schools and classrooms are tedious places, void of engagement and curiosity, it's quite possible that it's because we've inadvertently designed them to be that way.

In many ways, as we'll see, boring students to death may be an unintended consequence of a three-decade effort to grab American schools by the collar and shake them out of what, at the time, was seen as the scourge of US education: lackadaisical students, complacent teachers, and rampant mediocrity.

5

ENGINEERED FOR BOREDOM

In the early 1980s, American education stood at a crossroads. A Reagan administration report ominously titled *A Nation At Risk* had sounded the alarm that our schools had grown so complacent in accepting a "rising tide of mediocrity" for student learning that our national security hung in the balance. "If an unfriendly foreign power had attempted to impose on America the mediocre educational performance that exists today," the report intoned, "we might well have viewed it as an act of war" (National Commission on Excellence in Education, 1983).

Some rejected the report's hyperbolic rhetoric and accused the authors of selectively using data to create a "manufactured crisis" (Berliner & Biddle, 1995). Researchers at Sandia Laboratory in New Mexico, for example, dug into the same data (imagining, initially, that they would simply be validating the data and buttressing the report's conclusion) and arrived at the opposite conclusion: Student achievement had actually increased in every subgroup, but overall averages were flat or declining due to more (historically lower-performing) students being invited to take these tests. Those data, however, didn't see the light of day until years later (Carson et al., 1992) and, by then, policy makers on both sides of the aisle had busied themselves with bold efforts to "fix" our schools.

As a first step, 49 governors from across the US gathered in Charlottesville, Virginia, in 1989, and in a rare moment of bipartisan camaraderie agreed to set goals for dramatically improving the performance of America's schools, starting with raising the bar for students, which quickly translated into setting new, higher standards for learning. That much seemed to make sense. Yet as these things go, the standards themselves often reflected Mark Twain's quip about a camel being a horse created by committee. From the outset, the standards were often too vague and too voluminous to clarify for teachers what exactly they ought to be teaching; by one estimate, teaching all the standards contained in various state and national association documents would take 22 years (Marzano & Kendall, 1998).

Soon after, states rushed to adopt new tests to measure how well students were meeting the standards. Of course, with standards too numerous to teach, the tests quickly became the de facto curriculum for many schools and districts—a phenomenon known as "teaching to the test." Moreover, states increasingly took a "tough-love" approach with schools, adopting sanctions and rewards to incentivize them to take the new standards and assessments seriously—an approach codified into law with the passage of the No Child Left Behind Act in 2001.

THE PERFORMANCE PRESSURE COOKER

Basically, the prevailing theory of action behind these changes was this: Our schools (and by extension, the leaders, teachers, and students in them) had grown too lax and needed to be whipped back into shape. And because educators had supposedly gotten us into this mess in the first place, they couldn't be trusted with making schools better on their own, so states and federal officials needed to step up and demand results . . . or else. And so, we embarked down the path of using external motivators—namely, high-stakes testing (that is, assessments with consequences for poor performance, which eventually included school closures and the termination of principals and teachers) to stem the supposed "rising tide of mediocrity."

Over time, what began as testing in just a couple of subjects every few years as a "dipstick" measure of performance turned into annual assessments in multiple subjects. With so much riding on test scores, district administrators were anxious to know which schools might be headed for trouble so they could "support" them (or further ratchet up the pressure). School leaders also wanted to know which individual students and classrooms were struggling so they, too, could intervene with those students (which at times took the form of nudging them to drop out or classifying them as special needs so they could be exempted from taking the test). As a result of this proliferation of assessments, by 2014, students in many districts were taking 20 or more standardized tests per year (Lazarín, 2014).

To make sure everyone was fully paying attention to student performance on the tests, federal policy encouraged states to rate teacher and school leader performance using hypercomplex formulas that were often weighted heavily toward student performance on the state test. As an example, New York City's system for rating teacher performance was concocted from 32 variables and spit out numerical ratings that few people fully understood (Winerip, 2011).

Worse, test score-derived teacher ratings were often found to be grossly inaccurate, as researchers at Mathematica Policy Research discovered when they analyzed data for so-called "value-added" models that measured student performance year-over-year to assign a numeric value to teacher performance. They found that even when three years of data were used, the error rate was still 25 percent—meaning that for every three teachers correctly "measured," one was incorrectly rated (Schochet & Chiang, 2010).

Consider the unfortunate case of Pascale Mauclair, a sixth-grade teacher at highly rated P. S. 11 in Queens. When the New York City Department of Education released its Teacher Data Reports in February 2012, they ranked Mauclair as one of the city's worst teachers. There was just one problem—it wasn't true. From the start, the data were suspect: Of the seven sixth-grade teachers in P. S. 11, three received zero-percentile scores—unlikely in a school rated in the 94th percentile of the city's public schools. Mauclair taught both math and English language arts to, primarily, small classes of immigrant students who were learning English and entered her classroom at different times during the year, with some taking the exam after just a few months in her class. Because of the small class size, the number of her students who took the language arts assessment was below the minimum for publicly reporting scores. Her rating as a teacher was thus based solely on the results for the 11 students who took the mathematics exam, a small sample prone to distortions (Clawson, 2012). When ratings for individual teachers were released to the public, Mauclair, a veteran teacher held in high regard with her peers, found reporters from the *New York Post* at her door, asking her what it felt like to be the "worst teacher" in New York City.

So it's no surprise that teachers and principals alike report rising stress levels (MetLife, 2013), resulting in staff churn as they flee the profession (Strauss, 2015). At the same time, as test preparation has increasingly become the focus of classroom teaching, students drop out of school because they don't see how what they're learning (i.e., tidbits of information they're expected to regurgitate on a standardized test) is relevant to them (Bridgeland et al., 2006). Nonetheless, we respond by wishing they had more "grit" to power through all of the meaningless tasks we throw at them (Smith, 2014).

DIMINISHING RETURNS

Some might argue that some of this "shock treatment" was needed. After all, we live in a competitive global economy, so we must ensure our students can hold their own against their counterparts in other developing nations, right? Perhaps. Yet we might ask ourselves, Hold their own doing what exactly? Moreover, when we step back to examine the actual impact of three decades of attempts to "reform" schools, we see that across the US, as the shock of "get-tough" accountability wears off, states and districts have hit performance plateaus (Goodwin, 2015). A review of 17 years of performance data, for example, determined that adopting better standards and test-driven accountability resulted in some incremental performance gains among the lowest-achieving students in the lowest-performing states but did little to improve overall student performance (Goodman, 2012). And it remains unclear whether standards and test-driven accountability did anything to create more consistent, higher-quality instruction; one study a decade into such reform efforts found that only 7 percent of students benefited from having a strong teacher over three years (Pianta et al., 2007).

Thus, it may not be surprising that on international comparisons, despite the (arguably misguided) hand-wringing about our standing against other nations that sent us down this path, the US has seen only small increases as other nations have surpassed us (OECD, 2011), often by following very different paths to reform (Sahlberg, 2011). While we in the US have been using high-stakes testing to drive system improvements, leading performers such as the city of

Shanghai and the countries of Singapore and Finland have dramatically changed their focus from teaching facts to instilling deeper learning, from narrowly focused curricula to personalized learning for students, and away from high-stakes test performance as the sole determinant of school quality to the development of well-rounded graduates with highly honed cognitive and noncognitive skills and competencies (OECD, 2011). In a word, they've sought to help their students become curious.

STEPPING BACK TO ASK BIGGER QUESTIONS

So it seems that as a nation we've devoted countless resources, time, and energy to creating a Rube Goldberg-esque system of top-down reform while overlooking something vitally important: Do our students care about any of this at all? Case in point: A team of economists led by Steven Levitt (of *Freakonomics* fame) found that a simple $10 incentive—introduced on the day of the test—persuaded students to take the high-stakes tests more seriously and resulted in a performance bump equivalent to six months of additional learning (Levitt et al., 2012). Although Levitt and his team congratulated themselves for "proving" that external rewards could significantly boost student performance, it seems they inadvertently uncovered something else: how little effort students typically put into these tests in the first place—the very tests, mind you, by which their schools and teachers were often being held accountable.

Let that sink in for a moment: Not only are we using complex, convoluted, and inaccurate formulas for judging school and teacher performance, but the very basis of those measures—student scores on standardized tests—appears to be suspect, given that they can be so easily manipulated with a $10 bribe.

Still, some may ask, *But don't we need things like test score data to guide decision-making? After all, businesses must operate with an eye on the bottom line, so why not schools?* Yes, absolutely, schools need data and to focus on student learning. That much is true. It's also true that like any enterprise, schools should engage in continuous improvement, especially given the increasingly competitive global economy our students are entering and the fact that many students still fail to graduate from school or to develop the skills they need to thrive in a modern economy.

Yet even if we set aside for the moment the issue of whether standardized tests really measure student learning in any deep or meaningful way—including their ability to apply knowledge to solve complex problems, create and defend logical arguments, and employ critical thinking skills—we might step back and ask a larger question: How should we respond to these data? That is, how should we motivate people to use the data to do better?

The approach we've taken for the past three decades is predicated on the notion that good old-fashioned carrots and sticks work best. We might call this the "or else" approach. Get better, or else. Get the job done, or else you're fired. Meet your quota, or else forfeit your commission.

The trouble with this so-called business-minded approach is that a growing number of *businesses* are discovering that it doesn't motivate the right behaviors, especially when creativity and ingenuity are required to achieve better performance. In fact, Microsoft discovered that its "rank-and-yank" approach to performance evaluations—grading employees on a curve and dismissing the lowest performers—led to a decade of stagnation and lack of innovation (Warren, 2013). Meanwhile, many successful businesses, such as Gore-Tex, Toyota, Southwest Airlines, and Google, abandoned their "or-else" approaches and found it's far more motivating to provide people with a sense of purpose, increase their autonomy and personal responsibility, and encourage their growth as individuals (Deutschman, 2006).

Nationwide, a number of states and school districts have similarly begun to replace strictly punitive approaches to personnel management with "micro-credentialing" systems that let teachers set their own course for professional growth—by studying and developing skills in discrete areas of research-based teaching practices and receiving a "badge" or "micro-credential" upon demonstration of their proficiency to a peer-review committee. While these systems are still too new to have been subjected to rigorous research, a review of preliminary research (Demonte, 2017) reported positive effects for teacher engagement, who note that engaging in inquiry-based learning (i.e., being professionally curious) and sharing artifacts of their learning with colleagues has helped them to grow as professionals, which supports more-robust professional dialogue, climate, and culture in their schools.

Many educators aren't so fortunate to be in such encouraging environments, though. The stress many educators face right now inhibits their ability to create the kind of learning environments that foster curiosity and student engagement. In such environments, where educators' jobs hang in the balance if their students don't do well on tests that students themselves seemingly care little about, it's easy for teachers to feel as if student curiosity is a luxury they simply cannot afford. Unleashing student curiosity takes time—something teachers often feel is in short supply when facing an externally mandated press to cover many curricular standards before year's end.

While observing children interacting with curiosity boxes in their classrooms, Susan Engel (2015a) developed deep appreciation and sympathy for harried teachers, many of whom she saw under enormous pressure to cover vast amounts of material with "very specific objectives for each stretch of time," leading them to "put a great deal of effort into keeping children on task and reaching those objectives" (p. 636).

During their studies of talented teachers, Csikszentmihalyi and his colleagues (1993) observed much the same thing: Teachers weren't entirely to blame for disengaged students. The schools and classrooms they were observing in the early 1990s had just been introduced to the rapidly spreading "reform" of standards-based curricula and assessments. "An unfortunate by-product of the standardized curricula in most modern schools," they observed, "is the depreciation of the role of teacher to that of information technician" (p. 177). Many teachers in the study appeared to be mechanically plodding through the curriculum, teaching what must be taught with little effort to explain its meaning or purpose. On the other hand, in both Csikszentmihalyi's study and longitudinal studies of student motivation (Gottfried et al., 2001), even as high school students were reporting declining interest in their core subjects, they also reported rising interest in arts, music, and extracurricular pursuits (which, perhaps not incidentally, remained free from the yoke of standardized testing).

Consider another experiment that Susan Engel and her colleague Kellie Randall conducted with teachers who were tasked with guiding individual students through a science experiment supported by a worksheet (Engel & Randall, 2009). For one group of teachers and students, the researcher left the room by saying, "Have fun learning about science!"

For the other group, the researcher said, "Have fun doing the worksheet!"

As it turns out, Engel and Randall weren't studying students' responses to the science experiment, as teachers thought, but rather studying the teachers themselves. They had recruited students to serve as their confederates in the study, telling them beforehand to intentionally alter the experiment by picking up a piece of candy (instead of a raisin as directed on the worksheet) and dropping it into a liquid with the shrugging explanation, "I just wanted to see what would happen."

What happened at that point in the experiment was, indeed, interesting. The teachers who'd been given the parting thought to have fun *learning about science* were far more likely to encourage the students' further exploration, even suggesting other objects the students might drop into the liquid. Meanwhile, the second group of teachers, who had been told to have fun *doing the worksheet*, were more apt to try to get students back on task, redirecting them to the instructions on the worksheet and stifling their exploration.

If such a simple reframing of a single learning task could so profoundly impact how teachers interact with students in a laboratory experiment, we might wonder how regular reminders for teachers to cover everything on the test and stay on track with pacing guides is likely to influence how they interact with students and, in turn, suppress student curiosity. Conversely, we might wonder what regular reminders to *have fun learning* could do for creating classrooms where students and their curiosity can flourish.

Let's pause a moment to wonder what it might look like if we were to roll back the clock and return to the crossroads we faced as a nation in the 1980s. This time, instead of taking the path toward high-stakes testing, implementing hypercomplex formulas for measuring school and teacher performance, and castigating educators for failing to get their students to perform well on bubble-sheet exams, let's consider what might have been—and still could be—if we were to take a different path, one that starts with student curiosity.

REENGINEERING LEARNING WITH CURIOSITY IN MIND

Over the past few years, I've stood in front of educator audiences in locations around the world and posed the following riddle to them: What single factor drives the following positive outcomes?

- It's as important as intelligence in student achievement.
- It's as important as persistence in student achievement.
- It supports better job performance.
- It leads to better relationships.
- People with more of it have greater life satisfaction.
- It helps us live longer.
- It predicts leadership ability.

Rarely, if ever, do audiences arrive at the correct answer immediately. Usually, they cast about for a minute or two, offering responses like, Positivity? Grit? Motivation? Gratitude? When someone finally offers the right answer—curiosity—the crowd emits a drawn out *ahhh* of recognition. Why, yes, of course. *Curiosity.*

These interactions are not so different from what researchers find when they survey teachers. When asked to list important outcomes of learning off the tops of their heads, rarely, if ever, do teachers volunteer the concept of curiosity. Yet when they see it on a list, they give it high marks for something they hope to cultivate in students (Engel, 2015a). In short, teachers aren't opposed to curiosity; it's just been the furthest thing from their minds.

And who can blame them? As the previous chapter noted, public school teachers' performance assessments (and even pay) have increasingly been based on how well their students perform on high-stakes tests. In this pressure-cooker environment, who has the time to think about curiosity, let alone cultivate it? Thus, we appear to have perfectly engineered our education system to produce the results we're getting: student disengagement and waning curiosity the longer students stay in school.

SCHOOLING WITH CURIOSITY IN MIND

So what would it look like if we were to reengineer our schools and classrooms to produce different outcomes—namely, increased motivation and curiosity? What if, instead of applying the dismal science of economics to schools to pressure them to improve, we applied positive psychology to create a system of schools and classrooms that taps the innate power of student curiosity?

If that sounds like a bridge too far, it's really not. Already, a great many teachers *do* unleash student curiosity in their classrooms. Mihaly Csikszentmihalyi and his colleagues (1993), in fact, found this in their study of teenagers; while most classrooms were tedious environments, a few stood out as vibrant examples of engagement. In these classrooms, teachers sparked and maintained students' interest by modeling passion and enthusiasm for their subject areas, which sent a message to students that mathematics, art, or literature were full of fascinating and useful ideas worthy of pursuit. They also helped their students connect what they were learning to their own interests, lives, and long-term goals. One such insightful teacher, for example, launched a student's interest in a fashion design career when she told her student that, as a nonconformist, she might enjoy reading about another iconoclast: Coco Chanel.

Good teachers have always done this—taken the time to cultivate student curiosity and interest in what they're learning, just as my daughter's second-grade teacher did for her with an overnight science experiment that made her excited to go to school on a snowy morning. Interestingly, her teacher was a bit of an iconoclast himself. Years earlier, he'd helped to start a district-sponsored magnet school in which parents and teachers had come together to create an alternative approach to schooling, one that would focus on "sparking the intellectual curiosity of our students." Later, he found his way to our neighborhood public school, and Molly found herself in his class. It's likely no coincidence that while in his class, she not only experienced regular doses of curiosity but also began to appreciate curiosity as an admirable trait in herself and others. (For example, on Veterans Day, she proclaimed that veterans are "brave and always curious," which in her estimation was apparently the highest-possible compliment she could pay anyone.)

Years ago, at the advent of the standards-based education "reform" movement, a colleague and I facilitated focus groups of parents from across the US to glean their opinions on public education as well as the need for standards, testing, and accountability to improve educational outcomes (Goodwin, 2003). While listening to parents express their hopes and dreams for their children and what they wanted from their schools, it became clear that proficiency on standardized achievement tests was, at best, of marginal concern. Sure, they wanted to know that their students could read, write, and do math, but mostly, they wanted their kids to be in schools where they were safe, respected, and able to flourish—that is, to develop their own unique talents, abilities, and potential as human beings.

I emerged from those sessions wondering if the time, energy, and expense being poured into concocting a dizzyingly complex system of measures, sanctions, and rewards in the name of reform was worth it, especially when the results these systems were designed to create were largely deemed inconsequential for most parents and students. I returned to those thoughts on that snowy winter morning when I realized that—complex school-rating systems notwithstanding—my brief interaction with my daughter as she bounded down the stairs to breakfast spoke volumes about her school: She loves learning so much she hopes it's *not* a snow day.

I also found myself wondering what if that could be true for her every day? And on a larger scale, what if it could be true for every student every day? In other words, what if back in 2001 we had proclaimed that instead of leaving no child behind, we would seek to leave no child incurious? Or what if back in the 80s we had decided that if an unfriendly foreign power (to paraphrase the *Nation At Risk* report) had set out to sap our students of their curiosity (in the way they've been since), we would view *that* as an act of war? Where might we be now?

I know to some this all may sound fanciful and farfetched. Yet if we set curiosity as an aspirational goal and wonder together how we might help kids become and stay curious, we may see that it's not so farfetched after all, but well within our reach.

Glenroy Central Primary, Melbourne, Australia: Igniting Curiosity With Investigations

Afternoons are a special time at Glenroy Central Primary—a time when curiosity sweeps across the school. Right after lunch, the roughly 300 students in the K–6 school in a diverse, working-class neighborhood of Melbourne, Australia, dive into "investigations"—cross-curricular, inquiry-based learning experiences that engage students in exploring essential questions, such as these: How is weather unique every day? How has Earth's surface changed over time? What makes plants captivating? What can I invent?

Working in multigrade (K–2, 3–4, 5–6) teams, teachers guide students in hands-on experiments, critical thinking, and collaborative, project-based learning that integrate learning from multiple curricular areas (and content standards). For example, students explore how evaporation and precipitation create a water cycle, which in turn creates weather patterns, which when disrupted (e.g., in a drought) have significant impact on livestock, the agricultural economy, and people's livelihoods. Each investigation requires students to apply foundational knowledge in reading and mathematics they learn in the morning.

After each investigative unit, teachers compile artifacts of student learning into folders and posters that adorn the walls of the school. Teachers, who design and teach the units together, admit that creating the investigations has been a learning process for them, too. Finding questions big enough to explore yet not too obtuse requires constant tweaking and continuous improvement. Some units have worked better than expected, some fell flat at first but have been improved in later incarnations, and other were scrapped altogether. As confidence and enthusiasm have grown, students have had more input in the planning of the units. They are now working alongside teachers to build questions and create tasks and activities that drive the units where their curiosity leads them.

Initially, when the school principal, Jo Money, and her leadership team proposed letting students spend their afternoons indulging their curiosity through investigations, some teachers worried student performance might plummet on statewide achievement tests that are used to measure school performance in very public ways. So Money had to reassure them, "Let me worry about the tests. You worry about creating good learning experiences—and I think test scores will follow."

She was right. The school, where 80 percent of the students are in poverty and 55 percent speak English as a second language, saw its performance on the statewide assessment rise steadily. It now significantly outperforms similar schools on the state tests—with 42 and 58 percent of students demonstrating moderate and high growth in reading and 42 and 53 percent of students demonstrating moderate and high growth in mathematics, respectively.

Perhaps more importantly, student surveys of their connectedness to school, motivation to learn, and finding stimulation in learning have risen steadily as well, placing Glenroy Central in the top quartile of schools in the state of Victoria. They also report levels of mental health and well-being in the 80th percentile or above in all areas (Victoria State Government, 2018).

"So where did you start?" I asked Money while touring Glenroy Central in 2018.

(Continued)

Money, who came to Glenroy several years earlier in 2011, paused to consider my question, then offered, "Well, we started with trying to get students to attend school and with not having fights in the [school]yard anymore—to do that, we needed to get them interested in learning." In other words, Glenroy was no different than most schools when it embarked on its journey to building a curious school. It faced many of the same challenges as any school—and has certainly never been awash in resources or funding. Yet from the beginning, Money and her leadership team could see clearly what the school *could be* if they could unleash the power of student curiosity.

DESIGNING CURIOUS CLASSROOMS

In her book *The Fires in the Mind*, Kathleen Cushman (2010) poses a thought-provoking question to several teenagers: What does it take to get good—really good—at something? After dozens of interviews, she concludes that all students have a passion to learn something—to dig more deeply, explore, and learn about something of interest to them. In short, they're all naturally curious about something in their lives. Under the right conditions (which may include support from adults or, alternatively, adults staying out of the way), they're apt to fan an initial spark of interest into a flame of ongoing interest and, ultimately, a fire inside to become a lifelong learner.

These right conditions for curiosity also reflect, in many ways, the "unschooled" childhoods of Eleanor Roosevelt, Martin Luther King Jr., Winston Churchill, Mahatma Gandhi, Theodore Roosevelt, and other figures in history that Mildred Goertzel studied with her husband and son. In short, when it comes to unleashing kids' curiosity, there's no specific formula, checklist, or program (e.g., 30 Days to More Curious Kids!) to follow. Rather, we must focus on creating the right conditions for curiosity to flourish by keeping in mind a few important principles that emerge from research on student motivation and curiosity.

Curiosity Principle #1: Embrace Not Knowing

Kids are more curious when they know that it's OK to not know something—that is, to have a gap in their knowledge. Recall what Mary Ainsworth discovered about children whose mothers provided them with a "secure base" for exploration: Curiosity involves an element of risk-taking. We must delve into an area we know little about or where we feel incompetent. And we're more likely to do that when we feel safe to admit we don't know something. Thus, we need to help our kids see that it's OK to profess ignorance, yet a shame to profess indifference. We can do that by saying things like, "I *love* that question because it shows you're thinking deeply about this. How would you find an answer to it? When you do, let me know what you learn because I'm curious about it, too."

Curiosity Principle #2: Ask Fewer, but Deeper Questions

A thoughtful question or two can pique curiosity, but a bunch of them does not. As obvious as that sounds, the latter approach—peppering students with questions—appears to be common in education settings. A study of 18 college classes, for example, found that nearly 80 percent of the questions that professors asked during a lecture were low-level recall questions; 23 percent of them, in fact, required a simple yes or no answer. Moreover, the more questions the professors asked, the less complex their questions were (Larson & Lovelace, 2013). In contrast, the professors who asked a few thoughtful questions at critical junctures engaged students in much deeper levels of thinking, which suggests that asking kids to recall what they already know will do little to spark their curiosity, whereas encouraging them to build on what they know by surfacing new questions or gaps in their knowledge sustains their curiosity (see Tool 3 for some deeper-thinking questions to ask students).

Curiosity Principle #3: Replace Undirected Questions With Directed Ones

In *Ferris Bueller's Day Off,* Ben Stein parodies the consummate dull teacher by demonstrating a tried-and-true technique for boring kids to death—directing questions to no one in particular ("Anyone? . . . Anyone?") before answering his own questions (" . . . the Laffer curve"). Studies have shown that in most classrooms, a handful of students dominate the conversations, following something close to an 80/20 rule: 20 percent of students do

80 percent of the interacting with teachers (Jones, 1990). That means the other 80 percent of students may be doing little to think deeply or to feel any sort of curiosity about what they're learning. To engage students, replace undirected questions (posing a question to the entire class and waiting for voluntary answers) with directed questions (calling on individual students to answer questions; Walsh & Sattes, 2016). One such approach, called *numbered heads together*, groups students in teams of four to consider a response to a teacher question before calling on individuals (by number) to respond. It has been found to virtually eliminate student failure on subsequent content tests (Maheady et al., 1991).

Curiosity Principle #4: Use Questions to Provoke Thinking, Not Elicit Correct Answers

As noted earlier, sustained curiosity requires an element of courage—admitting our ignorance about something while feeling confident we can find the answer. Studies show that many struggling learners lack this courage and confidence; thus, they tend to avoid interacting with teachers out of fear of embarrassment (Kelly & Turner, 2009). Moreover, to further protect their self-esteem, they tend to disengage from learning, telling themselves it's not important. Quizzing kids to see who knows the answer can exacerbate many students' existing anxieties and disengagement. It's not surprising, then, that research finds that as whole-group instruction (an intimidating environment for low achievers) increases in middle school, high-achieving students participate more and low-achieving students participate less (Good et al., 1987). However, in classrooms where teachers pose questions to small groups that pique students' deep thinking, discussion, and curiosity—as well as carefully considering student responses instead of quickly sizing them up for accuracy—low-achieving students (and all students for that matter) become more engaged.

Curiosity Principle #5: Wait for It

Perhaps the most important thing adults can do to encourage kids' curiosity is something we've known for decades—ever since it emerged, somewhat accidentally, while researcher Mary Budd Rowe (1986) sat listening to hours of audio recordings of classrooms to evaluate the effects of a science curriculum on student dialogue.

While transcribing the conversations, she detected an interesting pattern. In most classrooms, teachers peppered students with questions, and students responded quickly with short, clipped answers. Yet in three classrooms, teachers let a long pause hang in the air after asking a question; after a few seconds to gather their thoughts, students responded with slow and deliberate answers. When Rowe began using a stopwatch to measure the pauses (which she called "wait time"), she found if they extended for three or more seconds and if teachers avoided cutting off students' responses, students were less apt to say, "I don't know," and more likely to support their responses with evidence. Students' responses were three to seven times longer than those of students in short-wait-time classrooms. Longer wait time also prompted more questions from students. In short, students demonstrated greater curiosity.

Curiosity Principle #6: Let Students Follow Their Curiosity

Because curiosity is personal—what one person finds interesting, another may not—we cannot force kids to be curious about a particular topic; rather, we need to give them some latitude to explore ideas and find their own interests in what they're learning. Even small choices in learning (what essay topic to write about or how to demonstrate their learning) have been shown to increase kids' motivation, performance, and willingness to take on challenging learning tasks (Patall et al., 2008)—a pattern similar to the childhood experiences of great figures in history who loved learning yet often hated school and thus did much of their learning beyond the classroom walls while guided by nurturing mentors and tutors. Theodore Roosevelt, for example, whose mother and governess taught him at home, would scour the nearby woods for dead specimens of mice, snakes, and birds to examine (National Park Service, n.d.). At school, Albert Einstein raced ahead of other students, teaching himself geometry and algebra and deriving his own method for proving the Pythagorean theorem (Isaacson, 2007). At home, family friend and tutor Max Talmud encouraged young Albert's interests in mathematics, philosophy, and science. In short, curiosity is more likely to flourish when kids are free to pursue their own interests alongside supportive adults who offer well-timed nudges to guide their exploration and keep their curiosity alive.

Melanie "Mel" Moore, a lead teacher of science at Joseph Banks Secondary College (a grade 7–12 school in Banksia Grove, Western Australia), encourages her students to capture their own curiosity questions on a "curiosity wall" in her classroom. When students have deeper questions about something they're learning (that might seem otherwise off-task or distracting to other students), they quietly get up from their desks and write the question on a poster provided on a classroom wall. At the end of the lesson, Moore reviews all of the students' questions and engages students in dialogue about the questions and/or uses them to guide future lessons.

Curiosity Principle #7: Go Play Outdoors

Nationwide, a growing number of preschool and early-childhood programs are encouraging kids to go outside and play; in the past six years alone, the number of early-childhood centers embracing learning in natural environments has increased fivefold (Williams, 2018). Many of these programs were inspired by Richard Louv's 2008 book *Last Child in the Woods*, which links increases in childhood problems like obesity, depression, and attention deficits to kids spending more time indoors (often interacting with media and technology), creating what Louv dubbed "nature-deficit disorder." Some studies suggest the best medicine for hyperactive or depressed kids may simply be a healthy dose of sunshine, fresh air, and unstructured playtime. For example, a study of 70 six- and seven-year-olds found that after controlling for other factors such as verbal ability, age, and household income, children who spent more time in unstructured, self-directed activities (playing with friends, camping, drawing, visiting libraries, reading) demonstrated greater ability to engage in self-directed thinking than those who spent more time in structured, adult-directed activities, such as organized sports, music lessons, or homework (Barker et al., 2014). These findings left the researchers wondering if a 50-year shift in how kids spend their time—away from unstructured, self-guided activities, like sandlot baseball and fishing in the creek, and toward structured, adult-led activities, like organized sports—may be impeding kids' ability to persist in self-directed learning—a critical component of curiosity.

A NEW CROSSROADS

To be clear, these seven design principles for curiosity aren't meant to suggest that children need no structure in their lives. To the contrary, when it comes to creating conditions for curiosity to flourish, we need to provide a balance between guidance and support from adults with freedom and latitude for learning—a happy medium that I observed one sunny day in April not too long ago when I found myself standing on a pool deck at Aptos High School in the hills above Monterey Bay in California.

All around the pool were droves of teenagers sporting white lab coats, business suits, and other "uniforms" to represent their teams in a regional underwater robotics competition. As I watched the teens feverishly readying their robots to be immersed underwater to engage in simulated "missions" based on real-life challenges that confront the US Coast Guard and other maritime agencies, I realized what was perhaps most remarkable about the entire scene: It was Saturday—no one *had* to be there. Yet the teens were all visibly pouring themselves into the task, reviewing notes taken from a 400-page, college-level textbook and perfecting their "sales pitches" for engineers from a nearby oceanographic institute who had been called in to judge the competition and "buy" the best robot.

In many ways, the whole experience demonstrated a perfect balance between adult guidance and student self-organization—a balance that sadly seems to have been overlooked in how schools across the US have responded to the latest "crisis" in education: the imminent threat of not having enough kids interested in science, technology, engineering, and mathematics (STEM, for short).

This latest call for school reform was sparked, in part, by *The New York Times* columnist Thomas Friedman, who returned from his travels in a competitive, crowded, and climate-change-ravaged world so convinced that the US is falling behind in the race to equip our students for the jobs of the future that he warned his daughters, "Finish your homework—people in China and India are starving for your jobs" (Friedman, 2005). Dire warnings from

Friedman and others, combined with test score data that seemed to show US students falling further behind their international peers in math and science, led business groups to sound the alarm about a "skills gap" in STEM fields, where they project a shortfall of 5 million workers by 2020.

Not everyone is convinced of these projections; some skeptics, like political scientist Andrew Hacker (2012), for example, insist it's yet another manufactured crisis, driven by business interests seeking to keep the number of guest-worker visas high so they can keep wages low. Other critics question whether pushing STEM on US kids is warranted, given that many countries that seemingly outperform the US in math and science place little or no emphasis on STEM. Nonetheless, if we accept that our students are apt to find themselves in a rapidly changing, increasingly competitive, high-tech world with no shortage of complex challenges, we might ask ourselves this: How can we help them master the knowledge and skills they'll need to survive in this uncertain future? One response would be to do more of what we've been doing: enrolling kids in STEM schools and programs. In theory, such programs and schools are supposed to get more students interested in and ready to pursue careers in STEM.

Yet in practice, that's not what's happening. Few kids who enroll in these schools emerge more interested in pursuing STEM careers than when they entered. For example, a study of 1,250 students in selective STEM schools found that students who entered these schools with only mild interest in STEM emerged no more likely to pursue STEM-related college coursework or careers (Subotnik et al., 2011).

A panel commissioned by the National Research Council (2011) to review research on STEM schools concluded that, in fact, these programs did little to develop students' interest or curiosity in these fields. That's likely because, as the panel noted, getting kids interested in STEM hinges on providing them with rich "research experiences in high school," including "scientific investigations and engineering design projects." To spark student interest in STEM, the panel noted, kids need to grapple with big ideas and "fundamental questions" about the natural world, so they learn to think like scientists. "However," the panel concluded, "this type of STEM instruction remains the exception in US schools" because all too often, our current assessment and accountability schemes, which rely heavily on multiple-choice items, limit the "content and complexity of what [states] test."

In other words, instead of helping kids think like scientists, many STEM programs fixate on helping them think like test-takers. For example, a study of 51 STEM academies in Texas found that while they trumpeted their ability to promote inquiry- and project-based learning, in reality most relied heavily on didactic instruction and explicit test preparation (Young et al., 2011).

A PATH LESS TRAVELED

It doesn't have to be this way, of course. We could choose a different path—one that focuses on engaging young people's curiosity in science, technology, engineering, and mathematics (and other subjects, for that matter) by taking a problem-solving approach akin to what students encounter in elite colleges such as Massachusetts Institute of Technology (MIT). In fact, in urban and high-tech enclaves across the US, a new generation of extracurricular math programs and competitions are cropping up that are producing world-class high school mathematicians and showing that kids of all backgrounds can master rigorous learning when adults challenge them with open-ended, multifaceted problems that students must apply deep learning to solve (Tyre, 2016).

Such an approach reflects not only the design principles of curiosity-driven learning described earlier in this chapter but also what I saw at the underwater robotics competition in California. In many ways, the magic of this experience was that it gave kids the opportunity to see, touch, and feel what they were learning and apply scientific concepts like buoyancy, water displacement, and electrical currents when designing their robots. The teens also brought their own personal interests to self-organized "companies" they had created to design, build, and sell the robots, assuming titles such as marketing director, project manager, science officer, engineer, chief financial officer, and CEO.

Adults were visible all around the school and pool deck that day, serving as mentors, coaches, and judges. Yet they weren't lecturing, quizzing, or demanding. Rather, they were simply nudging kids forward, fueling their curiosity. Nonetheless, the lessons the kids were learning were deep, complex, and motivating; I heard more than a few students express being starstruck in the company of engineers and scientists from Woods Hole Oceanographic Institute, where they hoped to work someday. In short, this "un-school" competition appeared to do what many STEM schools do not: get kids interested in STEM learning.

At this point in the book, I could sound the alarm that the lack of student curiosity in our schools is nearing crisis proportions, and if we don't solve it, other countries are going to "out-curious" us and leave our children leading meager lives of toil, trouble, and tedium. But I'm not going to do that.

For starters, our schools have been afflicted with too many crises as it is—often, with the implication that educators and schools are to blame for (or perhaps the only way to fix) yet another societal shortcoming. That's not very inspiring. Nor is it productive. As we'll see in a subsequent chapter, trying to frighten people into action is usually counterproductive. Moreover, curiosity doesn't work like that. We don't become curious because someone forces or frightens us into a state of curiosity; rather, we experience it because deep down, we *want* to be curious and find joy in exploring, investigating, and discovering something new.

So rather than using the rhetoric of crisis and urgency to send schools and educators frantically scrambling to make kids curious, measuring student curiosity ad nauseam, and fretting about kids who we just can't seem to make curious, let's come to the challenge of helping our kids be curious with a sense of optimism, hope, and wonder, considering what might be possible if we were to redirect our focus and energies toward creating places where kids can be curious. Let's imagine together how captivating and powerful it would be for our schools, classrooms, and kids' lives to be filled with curiosity—for our kids to pump their fists on a snowy morning because it's still a school day or to feel there's no better place to be on a Saturday than back at school for an underwater robotics competition. If we could do that—give our kids the gift of curiosity—not only would it likely make learning easier, deeper, and more joyful, but also, as we'll see in the rest of this book, it could make a great many other things about our lives and futures better, starting with creating better places to work, including better school environments.

A TOOL KIT FOR CREATING MORE CURIOUS CLASSROOMS

Creating a classroom where kids are brimming with curiosity doesn't happen overnight. Nor does curiosity emerge from simple gimmicks or quick fixes. Yet there *are* classrooms where students experience more curiosity and joy in learning. When you observe teachers in these classrooms, you see them using many strategies, often ones they've added to their repertoire over a period of years. Here are some of those strategies that you, too, can use in your classroom to begin creating environments where curiosity can flourish.

Tool 1: Build Learning Around Mystery and Suspense

Key idea: History, literature, and science are all full of mysteries. We should teach them.

The idea of grabbing student interest at the start of a lesson is not a new one. Years ago, Madeline Hunter encouraged teachers to launch lessons with an "anticipatory set" and McREL research (Dean et al., 2012) demonstrates the power of cueing learning with advance organizers. Sparking student curiosity at the beginning of a lesson is perhaps the most powerful way to launch a unit or lesson—both focusing and motivating student learning. Here are a few ways to spark student learning, drawn from research (Lowenstein, 1994):

Frame Learning as a Mystery

Mysteries are often at the heart of the study of science, history, and literature. People didn't always know, for example, that atoms were the basic building blocks of matter and still wonder how the Mayans disappeared and how gravity works. Yet we often rob students of the mystery that led to people to explore them in the first place, or we present things that remain uncertain as facts to memorize (e.g., the 10 causes of the fall of the Roman empire). So as you plan lessons and units, look for mysteries (e.g., how did the dinosaurs go extinct?), incongruities (e.g., how could a band of ragtag colonies defeat the most powerful empire in the world?), puzzles (e.g., how can I measure the area of a circle when there are no sides to multiply?), or "head scratchers" that create what's known as cognitive conflict (e.g., why does metal "feel" colder to the touch than wood?). Then, frame your lesson or units around those questions (of which there can be many).

Build Suspense in the Classroom

The reason we read books (or binge-watch television series) is because at each step along the way we want to find out what happens next. You can do the same thing in your classroom—keep students guessing what's coming next and wanting to come back for more. Here are some examples:

- I've placed a "mystery rock" in the closed box in front of the classroom. We're going to use our knowledge of geology to figure out where it belongs on the rock cycle, learn its key properties, including its mass and dimensions, to see if we can guess what it is.

- I've just received an important message, written entirely in Spanish, from a long-lost friend in Argentina. She says it's *muy importante*. I'm going to need your help reading it, as it contains lots of new vocabulary, irregular preterite tense verbs, and some colloquialisms that we're going to have to figure out together.

- Oh, no! Someone has gone back in time and altered American history, causing Stephen Douglas to be elected instead of Abraham Lincoln! Can you figure out what things have changed about the nation as a result? More importantly, we need to figure out what one critical event got altered, causing Douglas to get elected, so that we can go back and fix it!

- One of these rocks is an ordinary earth rock—the other, an extraterrestrial alien that has traveled here from outer space! Let's use what we've learned about meteors and scientific observation to figure out which is which.

Tool 2: Agree to Disagree

Key idea: Controversy can spark and sustain curiosity. Often, the best way to find controversy in a topic is to ask students to identify it themselves.

As noted earlier, Lowry and Johnson (1981) found that framing learning as a controversy (e.g., reintroduction of wolves into their natural habitat or debates around strip mining) helped students become so interested in these topics that they voluntarily gave up recess time to learn more about them. In contrast, students who were *discouraged* from debating and told to seek consensus became less interested in these topics. In today's divisive climate, you understandably may want to avoid hot-button issues. Yet instead of avoiding them, you can *use* them to teach important content, demonstrate critical thinking skills, and show students how to engage in civil discussion. Here are some examples:

- Most scientists agree climate change is real and caused by human activities, yet it continues to be debated. During this unit, we'll examine data, analyze arguments, and respectfully debate this issue. Then, you'll write a persuasive essay to defend your view.

- Until recently, the US imposed an economic embargo on Cuba. Did it work? Was the US right to impose it? Was it right to lift it? During this unit, we'll explore the history of Cuba, its revolution, and the economic and ethical implications of the embargo.

- The book we're going to read, *Catcher in the Rye* by J. D. Salinger, was banned in many places as a dangerous book. As we read it, I'll ask you to consider—and ultimately argue— whether it's inappropriate for teens or a timeless story that captures the angst of coming of age in modern society.

Younger students can learn through controversy as well. Consider these examples:

- A few years ago, Pluto lost its status as a planet. We're going to learn why astronomers made this decision—and why some people still argue Pluto ought to be a planet. At the end of our unit, we'll vote on what designation we believe Pluto should have.

- Some people say zoos are inhumane because they trap animals in unnatural conditions. Others note that animals raised in captivity often live longer, healthier lives than those in the wild. As we explore this debate, we'll learn important concepts such as predation, disease, and habitat.

- Some people say the book we just read, Shel Silverstein's *The Giving Tree*, is too sad for children to read. Others say it's not sad at all, but a *metaphor* about his mother. What do you think?

Can you use controversy to teach mathematics? After all, isn't math supposed to arrive at a *correct* answer, not a debatable one? As it turns out, research shows it's not only possible to use controversy to teach math, but doing so may be critical to help students gain deeper conceptual understanding of math concepts (Cobb et al., 1997). That's why, in fact, many new state standards encourage "argumentation and critique" in math classrooms. Here are some examples:

- Imagine two trees, one larger than the other, and five monkeys. How many different ways can the five monkeys be in the two trees? [Students debate different permutations, identifying new arrangements until all permutations are exhausted.]

- Review this geometric proof. The first three statements and proofs are provided in black. The next four, shown in red, are what an imaginary student wrote. Are his answers correct?

- You and your friends are selling popsicles. A box of 12 popsicles costs $4. On day one, you price popsicles at 50 cents apiece and sell 100. On day two, you raise the price to $1 apiece, but only sell 40. How would you set the price to make the most profit? [Small groups work on solutions, then engage in whole-classroom debate about how to arrive at an answer.]

Tool 3: Ask Questions to Keep Curiosity Alive

Key idea: Too many classroom questions are "guess-what's-in-the-teacher's-head" questions. The right questions keep curiosity alive.

It's estimated that teachers spend 35 to 50 percent of their time in classrooms asking questions, which adds up to the 300 to 400 questions per day (Levin & Long, 1981). Yet the majority of these questions are often low-level factual recall questions. So instead of facilitating active conversations and lively classroom debate, teachers wind up doing most of the talking, a handful of students respond, and the rest of the class tunes out. Good questions, though, can bring all students into the conversation and turn classrooms into vibrant learning environments where students explore ideas and become "infected" with the questioner's disease, learning to *ask* their own questions.

Here are a few of the kinds of questions teachers can ask to help students to identify and reflect on their learning gaps and begin to ask themselves questions about what they're learning:

- "Reflective" questions ask students to assess their own learning, including what's clear to them and what remains fuzzy (e.g., *What have you learned? What do you still need to know?*).

- "Connection" questions help students link new learning to existing knowledge (e.g., *What does this remind me of? What is this like that I've learned about before?*).

- "Picture this" questions ask students to visualize what they're learning and/or place themselves in different contexts (e.g., *We've been studying the Homestead Act. Imagine you're living in a sod house on the Great Plains. What would you cook for dinner? How would you and your family entertain yourselves at night? What parts of that life would be difficult? What might be better about it?*).

- "Stretch this" questions ask students to extrapolate what they're learning into new or even extreme situations (e.g., *How might you use the Pythagorean theorem to measure the height of a mountain or distance between two stars? Could you use the principle of water displacement to float a ship?*).

- "WWYD" questions ask students to think about "What would you do . . ." (e.g., *What would you do if you were Galileo and no one believed you? What would you do if you were Harry S. Truman and learned the atomic bomb had been developed and could be a swift, yet tragic end to World War II?*).

- "Different-lens" questions ask students to view their learning from a different perspective—for example, shifting a conversation about science to one about ethics, economics, society, philosophy, or the like (e.g., *Would it be right to use genetic engineering to bring wooly mammoths back to life? What are the economic causes of deforestation? Can scientific thinking make you happier?*).

- "Mash-up" questions ask students to consider two seemingly unrelated ideas or apply what they've just learned in a completely novel context (e.g., *What would your superhero powers be if you had the unique abilities of earthworms? How is* The Lord of the Flies *similar or dissimilar to* The Hunger Games? *How might an action hero use the principles of fulcrum and levers to escape from danger?*).

- "Non-questions" (a term coined by University of Melbourne professor John Munro, 2015) don't ask a question at all but rather prompt students to reflect upon, explain, analyze, or offer an opinion about what they're learning (e.g., *Describe the psychological and societal implications of most maps being drawn with north on top and out-of-scale depictions of land masses at higher latitudes; describe some ways you think people can be controlled by fate and others can operate with free will; write (and solve) a word problem that applies the quadratic formula to a real-life situation*).

PART III

CURIOSITY IN SCHOOL COMMUNITIES

Around here, we don't look backward for very long. We keep moving forward—opening up new doors and doing new things—because we're curious . . . and curiosity keeps leading us down new paths.

—Walt Disney

WHEN TEAMS LOSE
THEIR CURIOSITY

In the early 1990s, Motorola stood atop the handheld phone industry, dominating 30 percent of the global market for cell phones. It had just launched a new product, the StarTac, which was, by all accounts, an engineering marvel—the most compact phone ever invented. The clamshell design fit nicely into the front pocket of a pair of pants and promised to put an end to embarrassing "butt dialing." Yet, as history would show, even as Motorola reached these heady heights, its downfall had already begun.

At first, no one inside Motorola headquarters in Chicago paid much attention to the emerging threat—the advent of new digital cell phones. The "smart money" inside Motorola said digital networks would require multibillion-dollar investments in infrastructure that US carriers, like Sprint and Verizon, were loath to make. Moreover, carriers in the US could not agree on a uniform operating system, so anyone foolish enough to buy a digital phone would find that it might work in one locale but not another. Who would want that?

So Motorola stayed the course and kept cranking out analog phones. And why not? They were the big fish in the pond with no rivals . . . no *serious* ones, anyway. Sure, they knew that European carriers had agreed to upgrade their systems to support digital phones and that, up in frozen Finland, a company called Nokia had announced it would begin developing digital phone technologies, an announcement met with scorn at Motorola headquarters.

Nokia? How was that even pronounced? Besides, the Finnish company was best known for making rubber boots for fishermen and had just gone through a tumultuous upheaval with the suicide of its previous CEO. Its new leader hadn't come from the fast-paced world of technology at all but rather the staid, buttoned-up world of banking. A banker! The top brass at Motorola smugly assured themselves that their market dominance would continue well into the foreseeable future.

Then, a funny thing happened: Nokia's digital phones started to catch on—a trickle at first, then a steady stream, and eventually a torrent of sales. Its revenues quadrupled from $2.1 billion in 1993 to $8.7 billion in 1997. Soon, all of Europe adopted a digital standard for cell phones. By 1998, Nokia had gone from being nonexistent in the cell phone market to its number-one player.

How did Motorola respond? It chose to counter the threat by doubling down on its investment in analog phones.

What?! The head-scratching logic inside the Motorola headquarters was apparently this: *We're good at analog phones. We're successful at making analog phones. Past performance will predict future results. We ought to stick to our knitting.* And stick to their knitting they did, while watching their global market share shrink in half (Black & Gregersen, 2014).

BLUNDERS, BLIND SPOTS, AND BAD FIXES: INCURIOSITY AT WORK

The executives at Motorola were all smart, talented people, yet as business researchers J. Stewart Black and Hal Gregersen (2014) observed, they suffered from an affliction that's common to many groups—operating with faulty mental models that prevented them from seeing the obvious. Motorola executives are hardly alone in having blind spots, of course. Here's another cautionary tale from the business world: Blockbuster Video.

In 2004, it had 9,000 stores in 17 countries and millions of customers. It was awash in data, including customer surveys that told them, in no uncertain terms, that people *disliked* going to video stores and *hated* late fees. Moreover, they'd already seen the future of video rentals firsthand. A few years earlier, a Silicon Valley computer programmer, irate about paying a $40 late fee for the movie *Apollo 13*, hatched an idea for a new business—providing people with mail-order DVDs and no late fees, *ever*.

In the early days of the fledgling company, Netflix, its founder, Reed Hastings, actually offered to sell the entire company to Blockbuster, which turned him down. Hastings shrugged off their lack of interest and grew his company. Meanwhile, Blockbuster's customers left in droves, and it spent the ensuing years shuttering one store after another until it finally went bankrupt in 2010, a mere six years after its peak (Satell, 2014).

The executives at Blockbuster were also smart people with good information. However, like the executives at Motorola, their own mindsets and blind spots got in the way. Many of the them had learned about business while working at retailers like Walmart and 7-Eleven, so they figured the best fix was selling more candy in the checkout aisle. They also faced a high-pressure environment with shareholders demanding quick results—which may explain why the CEO's bold proposal to drop late fees and invest in a digital platform to rival Netflix's resulted in his fellow corporate officers, fearful of losing revenues, revolting and ousting him (Satell, 2014).

LAZY BRAINS AND GROUPTHINK

Blunders, blind spots, and bad fixes are common among businesses, organizations, and groups in general. Frequently, when people come together—be it in a company or a school—they do stupid things. That's likely due in no small part to how we tend to think about problems . . . or just as often, prefer not to think about them. As cognitive scientist Daniel Kahneman (2011) explains it, our brains essentially have two operating systems—a *fast thinking* brain, which operates quickly and automatically with little thought (it's what allows you to read the words in this sentence), and a *slow-thinking* brain, which requires attention and gets easily interrupted when our attention is diverted (it's what allows you to *comprehend* this sentence and read it critically). Our slow-thinking brain is generally in charge, but it's lazy—in Kahneman's (2011) words, our brains are most "comfortable in low-effort mode." Analyzing problems, peering around corners, considering other perspectives, surfacing and reexamining assumptions, and reflecting on what's working and what's not requires serious effort from our brains, which want to keep sliding back into low-effort mode. In other words, the trick isn't simply to be curious, it's to *stay* curious.

Sustaining our curiosity and keeping our brains throttled up to high-effort mode seems to be even more difficult when we're in groups—due to what sociologist William Whyte (1952) long ago labeled *groupthink*. Whyte observed a sort of inverse relationship between the number of people in a group and their ability to ask the right questions, make good decisions, and move forward with sound judgment. Somehow, two heads are not better than one. Often, the more heads in the mix, the worse the thinking becomes.

Whyte speculated that when we're in groups, we naturally want to fit in, so we seek to conform and to not rock the boat, even when we can see that our boat may be steaming toward an iceberg. Whyte observed groupthink in all walks of life—from companies, where he saw obeisance and group harmony rewarded, to academia, where he saw smart people grow reluctant to question the logic of mainstream thinking for fear of being ridiculed or drummed out of the profession.

When groups slide collectively into low-effort thinking, they're prone to a phenomenon that researchers at the Carnegie Foundation have coined *solutionitis*, or

> the propensity to jump quickly on a solution before fully understanding the exact problem to be solved. It is a form of groupthink in which a set of shared beliefs results in an incomplete analysis of the problem to be addressed and fuller consideration of the potential problem-solving alternatives. (Bryk et al., 2015, p. 24)

Examples of solutionitis are abundant in schools and districts; they include, for example,

- Spending billions on various forms of educational technology with, at best, only mixed results (Escueta et al., 2017).

- Using student achievement data to evaluate teacher performance only to discover these measures produce a one-in-four error rate and create wild swings in perceived teacher performance from one year to the next (Schochet & Chiang, 2010).

- Forcing students to enroll in advanced-placement classes in an effort to boost college preparation only to see steep increases in student failure on AP tests and dropout rates (Sanders & Palka, 2009).

- Spending billions to break large, urban high schools into small, autonomous schools (as the Bill and Melinda Gates Foundation did in the early 2000s) only to discover that "what struggling schools need more than autonomy is guidance" (Shaw, 2006, para. 8).

Avoiding solutionitis requires digging deeper to understand the real nature of a problem. For example, when Austin Independent School District (AISD) in Texas set out to tackle an intractable challenge—high rates of teachers, especially new ones, leaving the district—the obvious place to jump to a solution (better hiring and teacher-placement practices) turned out to be off-limits. Many changes to these practices would have required time-consuming and politically tumultuous changes in collective bargaining agreements and district policies. So they had to look elsewhere, digging deeper into the root causes of what was actually causing teachers to leave the district. As it turns out, they discovered that new teachers were often frustrated and dismayed about an overall dearth of constructive feedback from principals, which left them feeling as if they were sinking with no one throwing them a lifeline. So an obvious solution emerged: Improve principals' coaching and feedback skills (Bryk et al., 2015).

USING DATA AS A WINDOW (INTO OTHERS' PROBLEMS)

As it turns out, groupthink afflicts many school teams. In-depth case studies of school data team conversations, for example, found that instead of engaging in introspection and reflection about how to adjust teaching practices to improve student learning, teams often kept their brains in low-effort mode, looking at data in a mostly superficial way—focusing on, for example, how to present data differently or asking teachers to predict what percentage of kids might fall into various performance categories on an upcoming test (Horn et al., 2015). Other researchers have observed data teams simply going through the motions, mindlessly working through data discussion protocols with no introspection or identified changes in instruction before exclaiming with relief, "Yay, we're done!" (Datnow et al., 2013, p. 355).

In many ways, how school teams respond to data serves as something of a Rorschach inkblot test for schools: What they see and extract from data often reveals a lot about their own mindsets about students and schooling. For example, in one school, data team conversations focused mainly on sending "bubble kids" (who had just-below-proficient levels) to tutoring or after-school programs (Horn et al., 2015, p. 225). In other words, these teams peered straight through the data, with no self-reflection, to focus on what *someone else* ought to be doing, using the data as a *window* to peer into other people's problems—as opposed to a *mirror*, helping them to reflect on how they might change their own practices to support students.

In another school, teachers dug a bit more deeply into student performance data, examining questions students had missed to see which concepts they might be struggling to grasp—an improvement over pegging some kids for after-school help. Yet even as these teachers surfaced possible misconceptions, they landed on a strategy to "hit hard" the concept of dimensions to help students perform better on those test items in the future (Horn et al., 2015, p. 235)—basically, seeking to do more of the same, yet expect different results.

So instead of digging deeply into the data, asking thoughtful questions about where student learning might be breaking down, and posing "what-if" questions to surface what they could do differently, the two teams opted, respectively, to send bubble kids to an after-school program and double down on failed strategies. Neither reflected on their own practices (i.e., using data as a mirror), but instead were trapped in a sort of groupthink that told themselves, "We're OK; it's our students who are the problem."

CREATING COLLECTIVE CURIOSITY

In his book *How the Mighty Fall*, Jim Collins (2009) offers several cautionary tales of high-flying companies (including many profiled in his earlier books) that lost their way, fell into decline, and in a few cases, went bankrupt. Often, what fore-shadowed these companies' fall from greatness was an increase in unchallenged assumptions and a *decrease* in critical questions—such as Motorola overlooking the rise of digital phones or US drug manufacturer Merck peddling a pain reliever it knew to be ineffective and, worse, linked to heart attacks and strokes.

For Collins, these bad decisions reflect "hubris born of success," which is what happens when the rhetoric of success—believing success is the result of doing specific things—replaces penetrating understanding and insight—understanding *why* doing specific things works and when they might no longer work (Collins, 2009). In short, low-effort thinking replaces high-effort thinking, and groups begin to believe their success lies in a particular product or the way things have always been done. That hubris ("We're so great, we can do anything!") leads to the next stage of decline, which Collins calls "undisciplined pursuit of more"—more growth, more profits, more programs, more acclaim—and eventually to a third stage, "denial of risk and peril," during which people explain away bad data, ignore warning flags, and quash dissenting opinions.

Successful companies, organizations, and schools, on the other hand, continually strive to understand the *underlying principles* that make them successful and stick to those things. Such organizations demonstrate what Collins calls "disciplined creativity" as they explore and test new ideas. They also resist the slide into groupthink by continually asking *what* things are working, *why* they're working, and under what conditions they might no longer work. Basically, their success comes down to as a group, demonstrating sustained, *collective curiosity*.

The Walt Disney Company offers a case in point. In 2005, Bob Iger took over as CEO after a tumultuous decade during which Disney's image and stock priced had declined, erasing a third of its market value (Luscombe, 2018). Since that time, Disney's market valuation has grown fourfold, and its offerings have expanded to include ESPN, Pixar, 21st Century Fox, and the *Star Wars* and Marvel universes. Moreover, the company has changed with the changing times, adding new streaming services that are predicted to "disrupt the disrupters," Netflix and Amazon (Luscombe, 2018). Perhaps most importantly, it has strung together hit after hit at the box office, including the three top-grossing movies in 2018 (Luscombe, 2018).

So what's the key to Disney's success? Maybe more than anything else, it's that Iger understands his company's strengths—namely, that not executives, but creative teams drive its success. So he invests heavily in his creative personnel; he finds and recruits talented people and makes them feel supported and valued. He also encourages everyone to be honest about mistakes, learning from creative failures and moving forward. In short, what sets Disney apart from less successful companies is what sets any successful organization apart from others. As we'll see in the next chapter, it has everything to do with the people they hire (they're curious), those who lead them (also curious), and the conditions they create (helping everyone *stay* curious).

8

INQUIRE WITHIN

On a back road in Wyoming, a rancher leaned against a fence post, surveying his flock of sheep, when a luxury SUV pulled up. Its window lowered, and a man with an expensive suit, lacquered hair, and sunglasses leaned out and said, "Hey, I'll make you a bet."

"What's that, son?" asked the rancher, a blade of grass hanging from his lips.

"If I tell you the precise number of livestock in your herd, can I have one of them?"

The rancher considered the offer for a moment, shrugged, and replied, "Sure, give it a shot."

Gleefully, the man hopped out of the SUV, grabbed a laptop from the back seat, and flipped it open on the hood. He punched a few keys on the computer, and a satellite image of the hillside appeared on the screen. After a few more keystrokes, the computer ran an algorithm and rendered a number.

"Nine hundred forty-two," the man announced.

"By gum, you're right," the rancher replied and gestured to his herd. "Go ahead. Grab one."

"Any one of them?"

"Yup. A deal's a deal."

The man bounded over the fence, grabbed an animal, and returned to his car with it.

"How about a wager in return?" asked the rancher. "I bet my whole herd against your car if I can guess your profession."

The city slicker smiled. "You got yourself a deal."

"You're a consultant," the rancher offered without hesitation.

The stranger's jaw dropped. "How did you know?"

"Well, you came here uninvited, told me what I already know, and showed you don't know a whit about my business. And now," he pointed to the animal under the consultant's arm, "can I have my dog back?"

A consultant friend of mine shared that joke with me—a modern take on "greenhorn" humor, in which the rough-and-tumble realities of Western life cut a know-it-all city slicker down to size. In greenhorn humor, we delight in seeing the supercilious city slicker get his comeuppance—not because he's naïve, but rather *incurious*—he doesn't know what he doesn't know *and* doesn't care to know it. It feels like karma when a condescending jerk gets put in his place. So we might find it reassuring to know that something like karma appears to play out in the workplace, where fortune seems to smile on those who know what they don't know and are willing to learn.

WHEN CURIOSITY COMES TO WORK

We might start with this simple data point: Curious individuals appear to perform better on the job. A study of 233 service industry workers, for example, found that those who reported greater curiosity by responding positively to such statements as "I want to know more" and "New situations capture my attention" were better able to connect with coworkers, learn on the job, and adjust to new work environments. On top of that, it's likely no coincidence these same workers also received higher on-the-job performance ratings from their supervisors (Reio & Wiswell, 2000).

A similar pattern showed up in the automotive industry, where German researcher Patrick Mussel studied 320 entry-level workers in an automotive plant. First, he sized up their job-related curiosity (asking them to respond to survey statements such as "I am eager to learn" and "I carry on seeking information until I am able to understand complex issues"), then examined how supervisors rated employees on a variety of measures, including their ability to follow directions, work well with others, complete tasks independently, and work hard (Mussel, 2012). Across all these measures, Mussel found curious employees received higher ratings from supervisors, were more conscientious, more open to feedback and direction, got along better with their coworkers, and had higher overall job performance. In fact, curiosity was even more predictive of job performance than a variety of other factors that employers more commonly use to screen new employees, including intelligence, social skills, customer-service orientation, conscientiousness, and agreeableness.

In a subsequent study, Mussel and his colleagues sought to determine if curious people might also be better suited for jobs that require creative thinking and innovation. The research team asked nearly 500 people working in 188 different job categories to take the same 10-question survey of job-related curiosity. Using an instrument developed at the US Department of Labor, they also determined how much divergent thinking and/or innovation people needed to perform the essential duties of their jobs (Celik et al., 2016). By cross-tabulating these data sets, they found a clear link between curiosity and on-the-job innovation. In short, curious people were more likely to land (and perhaps stay in) jobs that required innovative or creative thinking.

In schools, creating an environment where teachers can be curious may have another benefit: stemming the tide of teachers leaving schools, especially new teachers, who leave the profession at alarmingly high rates. Anywhere from 17 percent (Gray & Taie, 2015) to 44 percent (Ingersoll et al., 2018) of teachers leave the job within four or five years—with a sizable group (10 percent or more) calling it quits after just one year (Gray & Taie, 2015). Sadly, in the US more than half of current teachers say they "don't seem to have as much enthusiasm now" as they did when they began the job (AFT, 2017, p. 2), and nearly half (48 percent) are looking for, or open to, new opportunities (McFeely, 2018).

What might encourage these teachers to stay? Studies suggest that simply providing them with a place to work that encourages collegial learning may be one of the best incentives schools or districts can offer to get teachers to stay. A statewide analysis of school climate and teacher retention data found, for example, that workplace conditions—including how often teachers receive constructive feedback for improvement, treat one another with mutual respect, and share a commitment to improving student outcomes—are better predictors of teacher retention than student income or demographics (Johnson et al., 2012). Simply stated, teachers don't leave poor *students*; they leave poor *organizational cultures*.

CURIOSITY THINKING ON THE JOB

Finally, it's worth considering the link between curiosity and critical thinking, or the ability to engage in "high-effort-mode" thinking—to analyze and evaluate data, reexamine opinions, and consider alternative viewpoints and courses of action. When surveyed, 343 executives of US companies said the skill deemed most important for new hires was "critical thinking and problem-solving" (identified by 72 percent of executives). Following were collaboration and teamwork (63 percent) and communication (54 percent; Labi, 2014). The skill *least* valued? Applied mathematics, believe it or not. In other words, employers aren't looking for people who merely score well on a math test (which, as you recall from previous chapters, is the focus of many STEM schools) but rather people who can use that knowledge to work with others to solve complex problems (which is more akin to what kids do at an underwater robotics competition).

All of this might prompt us to ask a larger question: What happens if companies, organizations, and schools fill their ranks with *curious* people? A two-year study of 28 companies by researchers at MIT's Sloan School of Management may provide an answer. It found that a company's "ideation rate"—that is, the number of employee-generated "winning ideas" that bubbled up to management for active development and implementation—was a key variable for predicting a company's growth and profitability (Minor et al., 2017). Specifically, companies with more than 300 "winning ideas" per 1,000 employees over a two-year time frame saw their profits grow at a higher rate than those with fewer than 100 winning ideas.

CURIOSITY STARTS AT THE TOP

In many ways, curiosity appears to start at the top; the most innovative companies and organizations have leaders who are curious themselves. A study of more than 300 entrepreneurs found that those who demonstrated greater *entrepreneurial curiosity*—a penchant for mentally stepping *outside* their own companies to understand the broader competitive landscape so they could, in turn, challenge the status quo *inside* their own companies to ensure they were keeping up with competitors—tended to be more innovative, curious thinkers themselves. Most notably, they reported frequently coming up with "novel ideas" and employing "original thinking" on the job, while finding less satisfaction in simply mastering a skill or doing a job exactly how they learned it (Peljko et al., 2017).

Perhaps not surprisingly, international executive search firm Egon Zehnder put curiosity at the top of its list of four key "hallmarks of leadership potential." From decades of studying effective executives, the firm found that the best leaders demonstrate "a penchant for seeking out new experiences, knowledge, and candid feedback and an openness to learning and change" (Fernández-Aráoz, 2014, "Better Hiring," para. 4). It advises clients to tease out potential leaders' curiosity by asking them interview questions such as, "What do you do to broaden your thinking, experience, or personal development?" and "What steps do you take to seek out the unknown?" In short, when trying to find a great leader, they advise organizations to "look for those who have . . . an insatiable curiosity that propels them to explore new ideas and avenues."

School researchers have noted that often the key variable in whether data teams engage in superficial groupthink—using data like a *window* to see what's wrong with other people versus a *mirror* to reflect on their own practices—comes down to one thing: a strong principal who clearly defines the purpose for using data (to reflect on and guide changes in instructional practice) and creates a noncompetitive "we feeling" in the school—making, for example, students' success in math everyone's responsibility, not just the math teachers' (Datnow et al., 2013, p. 353).

These strong leaders also created and modeled norms for data conversations, specifying what materials—and attitudes— teachers should bring to meetings, including how they would hold one another accountable, argue productively in a safe environment (adopting slogans like, "Whatever happens in your meeting, stays in your meeting"), and ensure conversations about students never turned to "nit-picking or trash talking"

(p. 354) but rather engaged in curiosity thinking and exploring new possibilities for teaching and learning.

HIRING CURIOSITY

So how can schools find and attract curious people to teach in them? A first step might be to acknowledge that the usual process for screening talent—sitting down with them and asking questions to "get to know them"—is pretty worthless. A meta-analysis of 85 years of research found that unstructured interviews, the go-to screening tool for many companies (and schools, for that matter), predict only about 14 percent of the variance in prospective candidates' eventual job performance—a few notches above reference checks (7 percent) and years of experience (3 percent; Schmidt & Hunter, 1998), but still pretty dismal.

According to this study, the best tool was a sample test—assessing candidates' performance on a real task they'd be asked to perform on the job—which predicted 29 percent of the variance in future job performance, followed by tests of cognitive ability (26 percent) and structured interviews (also 26 percent), in which candidates respond to consistent questions with their responses evaluated against criteria (often a rubric). The trouble, of course, is that most jobs, including teaching, are far more variable and complex than anything we can suss out through a test or structured interview. With that in mind, Jay Hardy, a researcher at Oregon State University, identified what he believes may be a better predictor of future job performance: curiosity. He studied the performance of 120 students in solving a complex task—in this case, a marketing problem that required both critical and creative thinking—and found that those with higher levels of curiosity (i.e., who expressed interest in "exploring unfamiliar topics and learning something new") performed better at this task. This prompted Hardy and his colleagues to advise companies to hire for curiosity and place curious people in roles that require creative and complex problem-solving (Hardy et al., 2017).

So what's the best way to hire and retain curious people? According to Kelsey Meyer, whose firm helps companies develop thought leaders and is, thus, on the lookout for curiosity in new hires, one easy way to gauge curiosity is to simply ask people what they've been curious about over the past few months—what new skill or knowledge they've learned or taught themselves. She also recommends giving people a task before an interview to see how deeply they research the challenge or what fresh perspectives they bring to it. Finally, encourage candidates to bring their own questions to the interview. "Curious people will ask original questions—period," she writes. "If someone either has no questions or asks canned questions like, 'What do you like about your job?' it's a big red flag" (Meyer, 2014, "Tips for Hiring Curious People," para. 5).

Kristen Hamilton, cofounder of Koru, which provides training for first-time job seekers, said her company has isolated seven key traits that correlate with on-the-job performance. One trait, as you might have guessed, is curiosity. In fact, Hamilton views curiosity as the wellspring of many other positive characteristics, including empathy, creativity, innovation, and the ability to learn quickly. How does Koru find curiosity in its candidates? Hamilton asks candidates to share the last time they "geeked out" about something—the last time they really dug into something to learn its every nuance. "If someone doesn't have that quality," she says, "if they don't need to learn every single detail of the topic in front of them—they're probably not going to reflect that level of engagement in their work, either" (First Round Review, n.d., "Curiosity," para. 2). Finally, like Meyer, she invites—and listens carefully to—the questions candidates ask, as they reveal a lot about a person's curiosity (or lack thereof).

HIRING THE BEST AND BRIGHTEST . . . OR MOST CURIOUS?

It's worth noting that Finland—often held up for supposedly hiring the "best and brightest" teachers—doesn't actually look for the *smartest* people to enter the profession but rather for people with a variety of other discriminating factors, including professional curiosity. Yes, it's true that in Finland, just *one in 10* applicants is accepted into teacher preparation programs—an acceptance rate on par with competitive universities in the US, such as Harvard, MIT, or Stanford; yet as Pasi Sahlberg (2018), former director general at the Finnish Ministry of Education and Culture and one of the key architects of the reforms in Finland, notes, Finland's preservice programs don't simply select the "best and brightest" but rather those with the *most potential* to become great teachers. Yes, applicants must score well on a subject-specific test, yet it's not simply the top scorers on the exam who are admitted into teacher preparation programs; half come from the middling range and 20 percent from the bottom quartile of scores on this exam. The Finnish system recognizes, as Sahlberg puts it, that the "academically strongest students are not necessarily the best teachers" (p. 63). Rather, the admissions process is also designed to find "young people who have passion to teach for life" (p. 63).

So in Finland, in addition to taking a subject-specific exam, aspiring teachers engage in a lengthy process that's designed to assess them in a more holistic way to fully understand their motivation for becoming a teacher. This includes a written test that asks them to analyze and interpret findings from five to eight education research articles they are provided six weeks in advance of the exam (NCEE, 2016). Next, they must interview with teacher preparation programs.

Although the interview process varies from one university to the next, here's how it unfolds at the University of Helsinki: Candidates engage in both an individual and a group interview. During the group interview, they engage in an authentic pedagogical task, such as reading and discussing a text related to teaching practice. During the discussion, professors watch how the candidates interact with one another, looking for indicators of the candidates' inquisitiveness, critical thinking abilities, and ability to work well with others.

This emphasis on teacher inquisitiveness is no accident—the preamble to Finland's national curriculum notes, in fact, that the "objective is to increase pupils' curiosity and motivation to learn, and to promote their activeness, self-direction, and creativity by offering interesting challenges and problems" (OECD, 2011, p. 123). Sahlberg, who served as chair of the task force that created the national science curriculum, noted that the curriculum was, in fact, inspired by what they heard the nation's business leaders wanted from graduates of its skills. A senior manager at Nokia, the company that outpaced Motorola, for example, told Sahlberg,

> If we hire a youngster who doesn't know all the mathematics or physics that is needed to work here, we have colleagues here

who can easily teach those things. But if I get somebody who doesn't know how to work with other people, how to think differently or how to create original ideas and somebody who is afraid of making a mistake, there is nothing we can do here. Do what you have to do to keep our education system up to date but don't take away [the] creativity and open-mindedness that we now have in our schools. (OECD, 2011, p. 122)

Ultimately, what Finland aims to create through its recruitment and support of teachers is a culture of curiosity in its schools. "It's so important that teachers maintain a culture of and love for curiosity in both themselves and their children," Sahlberg told an audience of teachers in Queensland, Australia, adding, "Curiosity leads to discovery and creativity, and they are the fundamental things of our time" (Queensland College of Teachers, n.d.).

So do schools simply need to bring curious people together and let them work their magic? Well, not exactly. As we'll see in the next chapter, schools can either suppress or supercharge curiosity, depending on prevalence of one simple factor: the quantity and quality of the questions they ask.

Alamanda College, Point Cook, Australia: A Curious School Starts With Curious Teachers

Alamanda College, a public K–9 school located in Point Cook, a fast-growing suburb to the south of Melbourne, Australia, unleashes student curiosity during a 90-minute block of independent learning right after lunch. Contrary to what one might expect, though, the post–lunch period is far from chaotic despite the lack of walls in an open-classroom environment. Instead, it bustles with the din of student activity. In each "classroom," students work independently on goals they've set for themselves and written down on notecards that sit perched in front of them to remind them—and keep them focused—on their goals. One card, for example, reads, "My goal in reading: To read smoothly and with expression." Another says, "I want to practice my spelling because I want to practice my capital letters."

(Continued)

(Continued)

Each student draws his or her learning goals from charts of learning progressions posted on the walls of classrooms. When students feel they've mastered their goals, they present their work to their teacher, who offers feedback and lets them know if they're ready to move on to the next goal on the chart. The students at Alamanda, notes principal Lyn Jobson, look forward to independent learning time. And behavior issues have become almost unheard of in the school—they are typically more prevalent among new students, who come from environments where they're accustomed to being controlled and often harbor some residual defiance, which soon melts away as they become acclimated to—and engaged with—independent learning.

Change, of course, is never easy, but rolling out an innovative approach to learning atop massive influxes in enrollment—the school mushroomed from 330 in 2013 to more than 2,900 by 2019—is a stunning achievement. How did Alamanda manage it?

Jobson offers an intriguing answer: She purposely sought teachers who were well-grounded in pedagogy and research but also experimental in their mindset and open to new ways of doing things—in a word, *curious*. For example, during the hiring process applicants bring exemplars of their work, such as teaching materials, student artifacts, or classroom videos, to share. As they share these materials, the interview team asks probing questions to tease out each applicant's thinking—not just *what* they do in classrooms, but *why* they do it, including the mental models and professional insights they bring to their teaching. Doing so provides clues as to whether prospective teachers are lifelong learners, passionate about teaching, open to new ideas, and comfortable working "outside the traditional" way of doing things.

In her experience, Jobson finds many teachers tend to be more comfortable with structures and routines than blue-sky thinking about "possibilities and opportunities." For example, when they initially engaged students in independent learning time, some teachers wanted more clarity on *how* exactly to guide students' independent study (Should they laminate goal cards? Type them? Ask students to write them?). Jobson whispered to me that she really didn't care *how* they did it, as long as they did it.

For Jobson, curiosity isn't simply all about exploring new ideas and flights of fancy, though. It's also about slowing down and taking the time to continually reflect on and refine what's working. "Rightly or wrongly," she adds, "I tend to take the artisan's perspective—that creativity and curiosity lead to a greater need to be precise and skilled." And when whole schools share that mindset, they collectively have the ability to say, "We're good. But how can we be better?"

CREATING CURIOUS ORGANIZATIONS

Few educators complain about having too little data. Over the past decade, schools and districts have developed, purchased, and integrated digital systems for warehousing all manner of student information—grades, attendance, behavior, demographic data, test scores, benchmark assessments, educator performance, classroom observations, technology use—the list goes on and on, leaving most schools awash in data.

Indeed, we now see many articles, reports, conference themes, and tech companies heralding the dawning of an era of "big data" in schools—in which supercomputers, aided by artificial intelligence and algorithms, will sift through staggering amounts of data and serve up new insights in order to, as Max Ventilla, founder of Alt-School, told *Education Week*, create a "different kind of universe in which schools can exist 30 years from now" (Herold, 2016, p. S4).

So far, it's unclear whether "big data" has done much to dramatically alter the universe of education or, frankly, if it ever will. For starters, a Bill and Melinda Gates Foundation-funded survey of 4,600 teachers has found that teachers are already overwhelmed with so much data that they find it difficult to "separate the signal from the noise" (2015, p. 18).

Moreover, as Finnish reformer Pasi Sahlberg (2018) has noted, "big data" may "promote transparency" and help to identify some general trends but "don't necessarily spark insight about the fundamental realities of teaching and learning in classrooms" (p. 29).

To unearth those secrets, he argues, you need "small data," such as checks for understanding, conversations with students, and regular classroom assessments—in short, "tiny clues about how students learn" (p. 38). Teachers have, of course, long used small data to guide teaching and learning. These data become even more powerful when teachers feel comfortable sharing them and digging into them to look for patterns, bright spots, and real-time improvements that can support students.

As we saw in the previous chapter, though, many schools struggle to do this, engaging, at best, in only superficial or perfunctory examination of their data. Moreover, as we've seen, people can still make bad decisions even when all the relevant facts or data are right in front of them. They can be awash in data, yet not put it to effective use—a seeming problem of "data, data everywhere and not a thought to think." In short, it's not simply a matter of having data or asking questions about data that makes the difference, but something else.

So what is it?

CULTIVATING COLLECTIVE CURIOSITY

As we'll see, it's largely the extent to which people collectively feel curious about the data in front of them—that is, the extent to which they ask better questions that lead to better insights, better actions, and better results. And how do they do that? Let's consider the following big ideas, or, keeping in the spirit of wondering curiosity, *musings*.

Musing #1: Embrace Mistake-Ology

One of the first reasons that people are often reluctant to embrace the use of data is that they fear a close examination of data will make them look bad, revealing poor implementation, gaps in student performance, shortcomings in their teaching—the list goes on and on. In short, people have little incentive to dig into data if doing so will only result in giving them a black eye.

From this, we extract our first musing for creating curious schools: Embrace mistake-ology. Yes, schools should strive for success and to deliver the very best possible results for students. But that's not always going to happen. Sometimes, even the best-laid plans fail. Also, people are human. They're bound to make mistakes. Sometimes, the challenge in front of us defies the first solution we try. Embracing mistake-ology means studying our mistakes to avoid making errors—which is to say, *repeated mistakes*. School leaders can set the tone for mistake-ology by admitting to their own mistakes—and even regularly celebrating them. "OK, so here's the biggest screw-up I made this month, and here's what I learned from it."

A study in the business world of the management styles of 142 CEOs of small companies found, in fact, that firms whose CEOs created a so-called *promotion* focus, encouraging innovation and new ideas, had significantly higher performance than companies whose CEOs created a *prevention* focus, cautiously fixated on preventing errors. A *prevention* focus, the researchers concluded, may work in stable, predictable environments where doing business as usual delivers results. Yet it tends to be ill-suited to dynamic environments, where new ideas and rapid change are essential. In rapidly changing environments, it's more important for leaders to create an open-minded *promotion* focus that encourages exploration and looking differently at problems rather than a cautious *prevention* focus that puts everyone on high alert to avoid mistakes (and often results in people making more of them or hiding them; Wallace et al., 2010).

As noted earlier, when education researchers observe school data team meetings going swimmingly—with teachers digging into data, respectfully questioning one another, and examining their own practices—they've noted a similar set of *promotion*-focused behaviors among school principals that made it safe for people to acknowledge—and learn from—their mistakes.

Musing #2: Focus on Getting Better, Not Being Best

Many leaders like to trumpet that their program/service/approach/ (fill in the blank) is the "best in class." Saying such things might instill school or district pride and make for a good slogan for parents on back-to-school night, but if people inside schools, districts, or any other organization actually believe all that hype, it can mark the beginning of their downfall—going back to what Jim Collins (2009) refers to as "hubris born of success." If we believe we're *great* when we're only *good*, we'll never get *better*. Soon, an "if-it-ain't-broke-don't-fix-it" attitude sets in, and curiosity walks out the door.

Leaders can encourage curiosity by keeping the focus on *getting better*, ensuring there are no sacred cows—no pet programs (including the leader's own), policies, or ways of "doing things around here" that cannot be reexamined or improved upon. This might include collective reflection on what's working to see if it can be done even better or with greater precision—for example, redesigning lessons to make them even more engaging or challenging, taking common formative assessments to the next level to measure and encourage critical thinking, or providing feedback to students that's both descriptive *and* encourages a growth mindset.

At the same time, a focus on getting better can also empower people to think outside the box to find or develop "everyday innovations" by, for example, creating inquiry-based learning projects, creating after-school clubs that tap into students' (and teachers') interests, or using technology to deliver more engaging learning opportunities for students—something people are less apt to do if they're told things are fine exactly as they are, so don't mess with them.

Musing #3: Use Data As a Mirror (Not a Window)

Leaders' own behavior and attitudes also determine whether schools approach data as a window (something they use to gaze out upon what someone else ought to be doing) or as a mirror (something they use to reflect on, and become curious about, what they themselves can do to make things better). In many ways, the ability to look at data honestly and have a frank conversation about it hinges on whether people are collectively able to view data with an *internal* or *external* locus of control. That is, do they approach data with an *internal* locus of control, believing they can positively influence student outcomes and, thus, view data as helpful feedback for improving processes, products, and strategies? Or do they view data with an *external* locus of control—chalking up disappointing student engagement or performance to external factors like poverty, family engagement, or lack of funding?

Decades of research have found that individuals with a strong internal locus are generally more successful in life—for example, they graduate from college at higher rates than those with an external locus of control (Richardson et al., 2012). Studies in the business world have found that small businesses whose CEOs had a strong internal locus of control performed at significantly higher levels (including being more likely to avoid bankruptcy) than those with CEOs who had an external locus of control (Boone et al., 2000). And studies in education have found that schools with a strong internal locus of control—something called "collective efficacy," or the belief among teachers that together they can positively influence student success—is more strongly correlated with student success than students' socioeconomic status (Goddard et al., 2015).

Leaders' attitudes and dispositions can permeate an organization—for better or worse—and influence how everyone looks at data and whether they bring intellectual curiosity to data team meetings. For example, when we have an external locus of control, we're more apt to view data as a *window*—revealing more about *others* than ourselves (our students are disengaged, their families are unsupportive, policy makers are placing unrealistic demands on us). If, on the other hand, we have an internal locus of control, we tend to view data as a *mirror*, or a reflection of our own practices. And only by reflecting on our practices, of course, can we hope to get any better.

All this likely goes a long way to explaining why so many schools struggle to use data effectively: It's less a matter of processes or protocols and more a matter of shared personal psychology—namely, how people within them view the world. Ultimately, whether schools use data as a mirror or window comes down to the conditions leaders create for people to be collectively *curious* or collectively *incurious*, which, in turn, reflects what we know about the conditions that help curiosity flourish: We're more prone to feel curious when we feel safe to take chances, experiment, and make mistakes.

Musing #4: Keep Wondering "What If"

Ultimately, better questions start at the top, with leaders communicating that questions are valued. That's important. The best leaders—those who encourage curiosity thinking among everyone in their schools—lead by asking questions, and lots of them.

Warren Berger interviewed the CEOs of several successful companies and found they have a key trait in common: insatiable curiosity. In fact, many of these leaders disrupted entire industries with a powerful *what-if* question—a question brimming with new possibilities:

- Square began with Jack Dorsey wondering *what if* his friend didn't have to lose a big sale to a customer simply because he couldn't accept a credit card payment? (Berger, 2015).

- Southwest Airlines similarly began with a guiding question: *What if* air travel was affordable for everyone?

- Apple disrupted the music industry by asking *what if* people could buy one song at a time?

What-if questions are powerful because they help us to imagine better realities and open doors to new possibilities rather than closing them. At times, such questions may seem wildly idealistic, reflecting a sort of childlike naïveté or wonder—what Berger calls a "beginner's-mind" approach to old problems and stubborn challenges. Great leaders use their curiosity to keep everyone open to new possibilities—even small ones—that less curious leaders might overlook. Curious leaders, for example, see bright spots in data, and instead of dismissing them as a temporary blip or fluke, they become curious about them, often turning them into stepping-stones to build something better.

In education, research shows effective principals not only tolerate "*what-if*" questions, but they actually take it upon themselves to ask them. As a McREL meta-analysis (Marzano et al., 2005) found, effective leaders, especially when guiding their schools through complex challenges, often exhibit behaviors such as these that encourage curiosity thinking:

- Challenge the status quo by asking what-if questions that paint a picture of a better future (operating as a "change agent") even while creating discontent with the current reality.

- Inspire people to innovate and take on challenges that may seem initially beyond their reach (helping to "optimize" performance).

- Encourage dissent and invite questions about purpose or logic of a change effort (demonstrate "flexibility").

As it turns out, visionary education leaders have a long history of reshaping schools and changing students' lives by asking their own *what-if* questions. Here are but a few examples:

- Wendy Kopp, founder of Teach for America, asked, *What if* we could recruit high-performing college grads to teach in high-need urban and rural schools?

- Dennis Littky, founder of Big Picture Learning, asked, *What if* the best way to keep kids in school was to get them *outside* school, to engage in real-world learning?

- Sugata Mitra transformed learning for thousands of children in abject poverty by asking, *What if* we installed computer kiosks in India's poorest slums?

- Salome Thomas-EL helped his urban students win national chess championships as well as graduate from high school and college by asking, *What if* we started a chess club?

Musing #5: Engage in "Revolving-Door" Thinking

In 1985, Andy Grove, then-president of Intel, faced a difficult decision: whether to abandon what had once been his company's bread-and-butter product line, memory chips. Japanese manufacturers had begun to cut deeply into Intel's market share with lower-priced products. Meanwhile, Intel had made a breakthrough with a different product: microprocessors, which it was selling to IBM to use in personal computers. The question before Intel was straightforward, but agonizing: Should they abandon memory chips and focus on memory processors? Abandoning a declining core business would be heart-wrenching, requiring laying off 7,000 people, nearly a third of Intel's workforce. Yet clinging to a failing product could sink the entire company and cause them to miss out on what, increasingly, was looking like the future of the business.

Basically, Grove found himself confronting the very same burn-the-ships question that many other leaders—including those at Motorola, Kodak, and Blockbuster—had faced, yet ultimately lacked the courage, insight, or curiosity to follow to its logical conclusion. After long hours of agonizing, Grove had an inspiration. As he recounts in his memoir *Only the*

Paranoid Survive (2010), he turned to Gordon Moore, with whom he ran the company, and asked,

> "If we got kicked out and the board brought in a new CEO, what do you think he would do?"
>
> Gordon answered without hesitation, "He would get us out of memories [memory chips]."
>
> I stared at him, numb, then said, "Why shouldn't you and I walk out the door, come back in, and do it ourselves?" (p. 89)

With the clarity provided by the "revolving-door test," Grove and Moore made the tough decision: They got out of the memory chip business. It proved to be an inspired choice. Abandoning the declining core business allowed Intel to focus on—and become the market leader of—the new market of microprocessors, thus securing the success of the business (and many people's jobs) for many years to come.

In a fast-changing world, sooner or later all leaders must employ the "revolving-door test," mentally stepping away from their organizations long enough to see the big picture with an outsider's (or even beginner's) perspective. Doing so reflects a whole different type of curiosity—a sort of "big-picture" curiosity and willingness to "go meta"—to step outside our own schools or districts and see them as others do, to understand what's really happening around us and reexamine our assumptions, and to embrace tough questions even if they lead us to painful realizations or uncomfortable insights, like the fact that what's worked for us in the past will no longer work in the future—be it film developing, clamshell analog phones, video stores or grouping students by age, teaching favorite lessons that have lost their relevance, or measuring student learning solely on a standardized test.

LEADING WITH QUESTIONS

Basically, what these musings add up to is that, contrary to the popular perception that leaders must have all the right answers, it's more important that they ask the right *questions*. Leading through questions, though, can be difficult for many leaders because, as Berger (2015) notes, it requires a "rare blend of humility and confidence"—being humble enough to know they don't have all the answers yet confident enough to admit it to others. Such humble confidence is crucial for modeling curiosity thinking. It also reflects what Jim Collins (2009) refers to as a "Level 5 leader"—the kind of leaders present in the most effective companies and organizations, who have gotten past their own egos and built "enduring greatness through a paradoxical blend of personal humility and professional will." As Collins writes, "Like inquisitive scientists, the best corporate leaders . . . remain students of their work, relentlessly asking questions—why, why, why?—and have an incurable compulsion to vacuum the brains of people they meet" (2009, p. 39).

Quite likely, some leaders may question the value of curiosity, worrying that asking (and permitting) too many questions could open a Pandora's box of people running around asking questions and challenging assumptions. Or they might think, *We already know what to do; we just need to do it.* They might assume they've already got a successful program, approach, or way of going about their business at hand; they just need to stay the course. Sometimes, they may be right . . . at least for a while.

Curiosity, though, isn't always a hammer for creative destruction. It can also guide our thinking in the other direction, helping us to "zoom in" to rediscover the core principles that made us successful in the past—and see how they could continue to make us successful (or help us be successful again) in the future. By looking more deeply, we might see, for example, that our success was never about a particular math program, reading curriculum, or inspired teacher or group of teachers but rather something more fundamental and replicable—perhaps the ability to set a high bar for students while supporting them, build strong connections with families and community members, or create supportive environments that help students feel they belong to something bigger than themselves. Such principles tend to be more timeless and grounded in what matters most, even as the outward trappings of what we do evolves in response to changing student needs, external pressures, and technologies.

OPENING NEW DOORS

Walt Disney seemed to understand all of this well. He never yoked his company to a single product—be it a movie, character, or even a place. Rather, he constantly reminded everyone around him that they were in business to do one thing: provide people with "magical moments."

Even as they created blockbuster movies and developed popular amusement parks, they never gave in to hubris ("We're so great, we can do anything!") or came to believe they had figured out the single *right way* to make movies, design amusement parks, or deliver entertainment. Instead, they kept reinventing themselves, finding new ways to make people happy even as their customers, competitors, and technology kept changing.

And they never got stuck in the past, largely because as Disney himself observed, "Around here we don't look backwards for very long. We keep moving forward, opening up new doors and doing new things, because we're curious . . . and curiosity keeps leading us down new paths." Indeed, as Bob Iger seemed to understand when he took over the company decades after Disney's death, the enduring "magic" of the Magic Kingdom appears to be that it bubbled out of an organization that consciously cultivated its own spirit of collective curiosity.

A TOOL KIT FOR UNLEASHING TEACHER CURIOSITY

In many ways, creating schools where *adults* feel curious reflects applying the same guiding principles of curiosity to school environments that we want to encourage teachers to apply to classrooms—creating safe places to explore, ask questions, reexamine assumptions, and experience the joy of learning. Here are some ways to apply those principles to begin creating a school climate and culture where curiosity can flourish.

Tool 4: Start Your Journey With Moral Purpose

Key idea: The best way to focus teachers on curiosity is to pique their own curiosity, starting with what's in their hearts—their moral purpose for being educators.

If you're a school leader feeling inspired to create curiosity in your school, that's great. A word of caution, though: Don't announce to your staff, "Hey, everyone, we're going to work on curiosity this year, so I want you all to get on board with this!" That's not how curiosity works. For starters, it's not a one-year initiative; it's something both deeper and more holistic than that. Nor does anyone become curious when it's foisted on them. Rather, we become curious because we're drawn into it—when we find something interesting and meaningful.

In McREL's experience working with schools across America (and the globe), we've found two things to be true. First, when introduced to (or reacquainted with) curiosity, teachers almost universally find it compelling and inspiring. Personally, I've yet to meet a teacher who, after learning about the tremendous benefits of curiosity, says, "Actually, I'd rather bore my students to death, thank you very much." Instead, thinking about unleashing curiosity in students often stirs something deep within educators, reminding them why they became educators in the first place.

So that's where we suggest you begin—by giving all staff in your school the opportunity to reconnect with *why* they chose to devote their lives to educating children. Here's a simple process, adapted from *Curiosity Works* (Goodwin et al., 2017), that you can use to create an atmosphere where people feel inspired, open to new possibilities, and curious themselves.

1. Invite small groups (5–6 persons) to provide a *written* response to the following question:
   - *Why did you become an educator/leader?*
2. Invite group members to pass their answers to the person on their left.
3. All members underline or circle words/phrases on the response they've received that resonate with them.
4. Repeat the process (re-underlining words, etc.) until statements are returned to their original owners.
5. Write key words/phrases on flip-chart paper for everyone to see.
6. Draft a single, shared response to the question.
7. Repeat the process with this question:
   - *What is your biggest hope for your students?*
8. After completing the second round (including writing key words/phrases on a flip chart), each small group develops a shared response to the following question:
   - *We believe our classroom/school should be a place where _____.*

We've facilitated these conversations with numerous schools and educators and have seen when educators reconnect with their "why" and share their best hopes for students, a strong sense of shared moral purpose soon emerges, which, as it turns out, reflects providing students with environments that encourage their curiosity to flourish.

Tool 5: Identify "Bright Spots" That Unleash Student Curiosity and Learning

Key idea: Students are likely already experiencing curiosity in your school (even if only in small ways). By discovering when they're curious, you can begin to make those kinds of learning experiences more frequent and commonplace.

Curiosity begins with a question—and a belief that the answer is out there, waiting to be found. So it's important to begin your journey with a question and also a "glass-half-full" perspective—one that recognizes students aren't *always* bored, disengaged, or unmotivated in your school. In any classroom, there are topics they find more interesting than others. And in any school, there are classes or activities they find more interesting than others.

With this in mind, you can start your journey to building a more curious school by inviting teachers to answer these questions:

- *When* are our students curious?
- *What* topics or subjects make them curious?
- What kind of *learning activities* spark and sustain their curiosity?

Record your answers on a flip chart or online document for everyone to see. Now, drawing upon what you've learned about curiosity in the previous chapters of this book, consider *why* each of the examples you've listed encourages student curiosity—that is, what's different about these learning activities than other, run-of-the-mill, less engaging activities; for example,

- Do they incorporate an element of mystery, cognitive conflict, controversy or suspense?
- Do they engage students in pursuing deeper questions? Asking their own questions?

- Do they allow students to pursue their own interests?

- Do they encourage students to solve meaningful, real-life challenges?

In addition, it's worth considering beyond the learning activity itself what might be different about the conditions you've created in the classrooms, extracurricular activities, or adult–student interactions when students are curious; for example,

- Do we encourage students to make—and learn from—mistakes?

- Do we encourage students to have a growth mindset or an internal locus of control?

- Do we give students opportunities to interact meaningfully with adults who get to know them and their interests?

Using the lists that you've now created, generate a list of guiding principles for sparking and sustaining student curiosity by using the following sentence stems:

- Our students are more curious when we engage them in learning that ____.

- Our students are more curious when we support them with/by ____.

We encourage you to synthesize your statements down to a manageable set (e.g., seven, plus or minus two) of statements you can make, which, in turn can drive a process of professional inquiry (see the following tool) through which you can consider how to make your "bright spots"—the things you already do well in your school to encourage student curiosity—more frequent and commonplace.

Tool 6: Design Inquiry-Driven Professional Learning

Key idea: Engaging teachers in inquiry-driven learning not only fuels their curiosity but also models for them how to create experiences that spark and sustain curiosity for their students.

If you've used the previous tools, you've likely surfaced some strategies for unleashing student curiosity in your school that are already present, yet not universal—for example, asking deeper questions during classroom discussions, challenging students with project-based learning activities, designing learning activities around mysteries or driving questions, or helping students develop a growth mindset so they're willing to tackle complex problems and learn from mistakes.

At this point, though, instead of directing everyone to engage in professional development around one of these strategies, you'll be more apt to build a curious school by inviting teachers to identify a focus for their own professional learning, framed as a question. In schoolwide, grade-, or department-level meetings (depending on the size and needs of your school), invite teachers to develop a "problem-of-practice" question—one they will explore and develop a response to over a specified period of time (e.g., six weeks to a semester). You may find these frames helpful:

- How can we consistently apply the curiosity-sparking/-sustaining strategy we've identified (or with greater frequency and precision in our teaching?)

- What can we do to provide more students with the curiosity-supporting condition we identified?

Basically, groups should frame a question they can answer with data (e.g., student artifacts, classroom observations, common formative assessments) in a manageable period of time. With this in mind, an inquiry should include the following elements:

- A brief investigation. Over a short period (e.g., two to three weeks), investigate research-based guidance (e.g., articles, videos, book chapters) on a particular strategy and/or condition you can address in a rapid improvement cycle. Be sure to focus on something manageable you can embed in classrooms in a matter of weeks (e.g., better questions, wait time, goal setting, etc.).

- Clarify the solution and set goals. After identifying what strategy/condition you'll embed, create a rubric to clarify what *ideal* (and adequate and inadequate) use of the strategy or condition will look like. Next, identify what data you'll use to track the results of your rapid-improvement cycle effort (e.g., classroom participation, work samples, engagement surveys)— in essence, generate a hypothesis to test (i.e., if we do X well, Y should happen).

- Use peer feedback to fine-tune implementation. As you apply the new strategy or condition, observe each other's classrooms to help one another reflect and refine what you're doing. The point here isn't to evaluate your colleagues (e.g., "You didn't do that right") but rather to help them see what's happening (e.g., "I saw every student really engaged in that activity, though some seem confused about the purpose"). After sharing feedback, reflect on how to refine the strategy or condition.

- Collect and analyze your data. This is perhaps the most important part of the process—taking stock of how it worked for students—returning to your theory of action to see if the strategy you used or condition you created resulted in your desired outcomes.

- Plan next steps. Learning doesn't end here, of course. Rather, like curiosity itself, answering one question should lead to a new set of questions—what else can we do to encourage student curiosity? You may decide you need to further refine what you've been doing, go deeper with it, or incorporate additional strategies or conditions.

You can learn more about this process in *Curiosity Works* (Goodwin et al., 2017).

PART IV

CURIOUS AT HEART

You never really understand a person until you consider things from his point of view—until you climb into his skin and walk around in it.

—Atticus Finch in Harper Lee's novel,
To Kill a Mockingbird

10

ALONE TOGETHER

If you'd been alive at the turn of the last century, you likely would've lived in a rural area, where you'd interact with only a few people every day. You'd talk to your family and maybe chat with a neighbor over the fence. On weekends, you might venture to town and converse with the local shopkeeper and fellow parishioners at your place of worship—all people you'd have known your whole life. As a child, you probably would attend school in a one-room schoolhouse with your siblings, cousins, and neighbors—people you'd known your whole life. While few, your social interactions would have been deep, authentic, and self-regulated; in a small town or rural countryside, there would be no cloak of anonymity—you couldn't flip someone the bird from your horse carriage and not expect it to damage your standing in the community. Only occasionally might you interact with someone you *didn't* know: a stranger.

However, with the dawning of the industrial age and increasing urbanization of our society, all that began to change, as Susan Cain (2013) describes in her illuminating book, *Quiet: The Power of Introverts in a World That Can't Stop Talking*. At the start of the 20th century, many people suddenly found themselves thrust into a world in which most of their social interactions were with complete strangers. That created a great deal of anxiety for many, especially, as Cain argues, for introverts who turned into avid consumers of a new industry of self-help books and seminars aimed at helping them develop more outgoing personalities, including the ability to be "fascinating," "magnetic," "forceful," and "glowing"—a far cry from 19th century self-help books that encouraged "citizenship," "duty," "Golden deeds," "honor," "reputation," and "morals" (Cain, 2013).

REPLACING INTERPERSONAL WITH IMPERSONAL

Nowadays, of course, most of us find nothing strange about interacting with *strangers*—they're all around us: at coffee shops, grocery stores, stoplights, and residences in close proximity to us—including in the same apartment building or just around the block from us. In fact, for the overwhelming majority of Americans who now live in urban areas, we find it *strange* to see a *familiar face* in a public place. As a result, the modern world, in Cain's view, has become an extrovert's paradise, a place where those who are adept at fist bumping and small talk thrive, while those prone to introspection, quiet conversation, and empathy may feel disquieted and overwhelmed.

Patricia Greenfield, a researcher at UCLA, documented a similar, dramatic shift in our culture by using the Google Books NGram Viewer to analyze words used in thousands of texts published between 1800 and 2000—a period of time during which the US population went from being predominantly rural (with 94 percent of Americans living in sparsely populated areas) to predominantly urban (with 79 percent living in densely populated areas; Greenfield, 2012). The mosaic of words in print paints a picture of a culture moving from communal obligation toward individual self-determination: For instance, words like *choose* and *decide* increased fivefold, while words like *duty* and *obliged* dropped to a third of previous levels; at the same time, *give* became less frequent while *get* became more prevalent, and words associated with personal emotion (e.g., *feel*) eclipsed those associated with interpersonal action (e.g., *act*, *deeds*). Greenfield also saw a sharp decline in other-centered words, like *obedience*, *authority*, *belong*, and *pray* and a steep rise in self-centered words like *individual*, *ego*, *personal*, and *self*. This sweeping change in the zeitgeist may explain the societal reaction (or *over*reaction) to a tragic event in New York City in the mid-1960s, which, in turn, spawned a whole new field of research.

BYSTANDERS IN ONE ANOTHER'S LIVES

Shortly after 3 a.m. on March 13, 1964, Kitty Genovese, a 28-year-old bar manager, was brutally stabbed to death outside her apartment in the Kew Gardens neighborhood of Queens. In the first retelling of the incident (Gansberg, 1964), her cries for help echoed across the quiet neighborhood, yet no one came to her defense. Afterward, the police said some 38 people had heard Kitty's cries for help yet failed to confront the attacker, come to her aid, or alert authorities. One told a newspaper reporter, "I didn't want to get involved."

As it turns out, the circumstances of Kitty's death were sensationalized —in reality, only a half-dozen or so people (not 38) heard her cries for help, and many did, in fact, call the police (Merry, 2016). Those facts, however, did not emerge until years later, so at the time, the seeming indifference of her witnesses shocked a nation and led to the creation of the 911 emergency system. And amid the outrage and soul searching, researchers began to delve into why people turn a blind eye to the suffering of fellow humans. Soon, they coined a new term, *the bystander effect*, to explain why people in a crowd seem to find it easier to ignore others' cries for help.

Sociologists also began to wonder if the incident might reflect a darker malaise in the heart of our national psyche— manifestations of what, decades earlier, Louis Wirth, a member of the renowned Chicago School of Sociology, had labeled the "urban personality." A fundamental paradox of urban living, Wirth observed, is *being alone together*. City dwellers, he observed, live in "frequent close physical contact," yet are separated by "great social distance," leaving them feeling socially detached, which, in turn, gives "rise to loneliness." Because urbanites rub shoulders with more strangers than they can relate to as individuals, it's easy to grow increasingly detached and callous to one another's humanity. As a result, something inside them slowly dies—something we might call empathy, compassion, or interpersonal curiosity.

All of this reflects, according to Greenfield, the massive sea change in our culture over the past 200 years: moving away from what German sociologists called *gemeinschaft*, or *community*—mostly rural areas that relied on interpersonal dependence and placed a high value on duty, religion, and group welfare—and toward *gesellschaft*, or *society*—secularized urban areas where people interact mostly via impersonal commerce and place a high value on individual freedom and the accumulation of wealth—in short, the welfare of one's own self.

LOOKING FOR DIFFERENCES IN INDIFFERENCE

In the years following Kitty Genovese's sensationalized murder, psychologists began to test the bystander effect on street corners across the US, the UK, and Australia to see if they might detect differences in the helpfulness of people who live in small towns versus midsized cities or large, urban areas. Usually, the experiments would go like this: A stranger standing on a street corner would make a simple request of passersby, such as asking for directions or the time of day. At other times, they might make more serious requests, such as feigning injury and pleading for help.

Over the course of dozens of studies, an interesting pattern emerged. A meta-analysis of these studies found that while generally speaking, "country people are more helpful than city people," people in the smallest communities (fewer than 5,000 people) seemed to be wariest of, and most reluctant to help, strangers. Helpfulness, in fact, generally rose with the population up to a threshold of 300,000 people—at which point, kindness toward strangers appeared to drop sharply (Steblay, 1987). In general, what these studies have found is that the more people in a crowd, the more likely individuals are to melt into the crowd and avoid helping others in distress (Fischer et. al, 2011).

ARE WE BECOMING LESS EMPATHETIC?

Following a similar line of inquiry, for the past four decades researchers have been surveying college students using a scientifically validated 28-item questionnaire designed to measure four different types of intellectual and emotional empathy:

- Empathic concern (e.g., "I often have tender, concerned feelings for people less fortunate than me")

- Perspective taking (e.g., "I try to look at everybody's side of a disagreement before I make a decision")

- Fantasy (e.g., "I really get involved with the feelings of the characters in a novel")

- Personal distress (e.g., "When I see someone who badly needs help in an emergency, I go to pieces")

The first two measures—empathic concern and perspective taking—are important because both have been strongly correlated with a host of positive outcomes: People who demonstrate empathic concern are less likely to demonstrate socially dysfunctional traits like boasting, verbal aggression, and loneliness. They're also more likely to volunteer, return incorrect change, let somebody cut ahead of them in line, carry a stranger's belongings, and donate money to charity. Similarly, people high in perspective taking are more likely to volunteer, donate to charity, and have high self-esteem, and they are less likely to demonstrate socially dysfunctional behaviors. Moreover, schools where students rate high in both empathic concern and perspective taking experience less bullying.

Conversely, people who rate low on empathic concern and perspective taking are more likely to demonstrate aggressive behavior while inebriated and commit sexual offenses and child abuse, leading some researchers to conclude that these scales may be among the best available predictors of criminal behavior. And as it turns out, the latter two measures—fantasy and personal distress—are both correlated with antisocial behaviors, including narcissism and avoiding others in distress.

Here's where there's seeming cause for concern: Over the past four decades, these surveys of young people have detected a 48 percent decrease in empathic concern and a 34 percent drop in perspective taking. Meanwhile, the dysfunctional forms of empathy—fantasy and personal distress—remained unchanged (Konrath et al., 2011). Although there's no scientific way to isolate the exact cause of these declines, research points to a likely culprit that has seemingly spawned yet a sea change in our culture—one that appears to be as dramatic as the shift from country to city life—especially for young people.

iLONELY

Jean Twenge (2018) has devoted her career to studying large, longitudinal datasets that track thousands of young people's responses, over time, to surveys about their attitudes, personal preferences, and beliefs. During her years of scrutinizing trend lines in these charts, she'd grown accustomed to seeing "hills slowly growing into peaks," as over a decade or longer, cultural changes "that started with a few young people swelled to many" (p. 4). She'd seen, for example, a spike in individualism and materialism as millennials came of age and risky behaviors persisting among twenty-somethings as Gen Xers extended their adolescence well past the age when most boomers had settled down.

"But around 2012," she notes, "I started seeing large, abrupt shifts in teens' behaviors and emotional states" (2018, p. 4). Lines on graphs that had once been gentle slopes, rolling hills, and valleys suddenly turned into "steep mountains" and "sheer cliffs" (p. 4)—including steep rises in teens expressing loneliness, mental depression, and suicidal thoughts while their happiness, interpersonal interactions, and life satisfaction fell off a cliff. "In all my analyses of generational data—some of it reaching back to the 1930s—I had never seen anything like it," Twenge wrote (p. 4).

At first, she thought they might just be "random blips" in the data that would disappear after a year or two (p. 5). But they didn't—in fact, they worsened; the mountains grew steeper and cliffs sharper. What would cause such a broad, sudden shift in teens' attitudes between 2011 and 2012? Like a mystery detective, Twenge considered —and eliminated—other suspects, like a weakened economy, which didn't match the data, as the Great Recession had occurred a few years earlier.

Then, it hit her. Smartphones. Between the years 2011 and 2012, the majority of American teens—at all socioeconomic levels— had come into possession of smartphones—mobile phones and tablets that could access the Internet. Smartphones, in turn, led to a second cultural tsunami: social media. Together, smartphones and social media transformed the lives of teenagers, changing how they communicate (mostly digitally) and spend their free time (usually at home, on their phones). According to a study from the Pew Research Center, some 95 percent of teens in 2018 had a smartphone, and 45 percent reported using the Internet "almost constantly"—twice the number from just four years earlier (Anderson & Jiang, 2018). Smartphone use is equally high regardless of income—93 percent of teens with a family income below $30,000 per year report having a phone versus 97 percent for teens whose family income is above $75,000 (Anderson & Jiang, 2018).

Overall, this seismic shift in attitudes, perceptions, and use of personal time among young people has been so pronounced that Twenge sees the advent of the smartphone as a clear marker for the beginning of a new generation, which she calls iGen. This generation, born after 1995, is entering our schools with markedly different behaviors and needs than previous generations. Some of these changes are positive. For example, today's youth are more tolerant and less apt to engage in risky behaviors than previous generations.

Nonetheless, as Twenge puts it, "The complete dominance of the smartphone among teens has had ripple effects across every area of iGeners' lives, from their social interactions to their mental health." Consider, for example, the following data:

- They're less likely to spend time together. Twelfth graders in 2015 went out *less often* with friends than *eighth graders* did just six years earlier, in 2009.

- They're less likely to drive a car. More than a quarter of iGen twelfth graders don't have a driver's license, whereas nearly all boomers had a license at the same age.

- They're less apt to engage in activities linked to greater well-being. Specifically, they're less likely to engage in sports or exercise, religious activities, reading books, and interacting with others in person.

Basically, today's young people appear to have more social "connections" yet fewer genuine relationships than previous generations, which Twenge suspects is having a negative effect on their well-being and mental health. For example, after analyzing data from more than 500,000 teens she and her colleagues (Twenge et al., 2018) noted that teens' risks of mental depression and suicidal thoughts began to increase with two hours of screen time per day and spike sharply upward with four or more hours of screen time per day.

These data are concerning because according to a study from nonprofit media watchdog Common Sense Media the average teen spends *more than five hours per day* in front of screens—even more for low-income teens, who spend, on average, eight hours and seven minutes per day in front of screens (on their phones, tablets, or TVs) versus five hours and 42 minutes per day for wealthier teens (Rideout, 2018). Indeed, whereas a few years ago researchers worried that rich kids had more access to technology than poor kids, a new, inverted digital divide seems to be at play—with poor kids spending more time online and in front of screens than rich ones.

In light of all these data, it's perhaps not surprising that a national study of 20,000 Americans from health insurer Cigna (2018) found that loneliness has reached "epidemic" proportions in America, with nearly half of those surveyed reporting feeling sometimes or frequently lonely. Most strikingly, young adults (between 18 and 22) were the loneliest group surveyed—lonelier, even, than elderly Americans (over the age of 72). Let that soak in for a moment: At the very time we imagine young people are living one long episode of the TV series *Friends*—happily squeezed together in college dormitories, shared apartments, and crowded coffee shops—they're apt to report *greater loneliness* than their grandparents.

Arguably, as community ties have weakened and social media has left our students feeling, at best, like bystanders in others' lives, they may be in desperate need of restoring another kind of curiosity in their lives—namely, curiosity about other people. In the following chapters, we'll explore how we can help students restore what may have been lost in the age of smartphones and weakened social ties by unleashing their *interpersonal* curiosity.

GOING COLD TURKEY

For the British teens who subjected themselves to a new type of detox program—one that's becoming increasingly common in the UK, the US, and elsewhere—going "cold turkey" spawned a predictable wave of emotions: denial, resentment, and anger. Gradually, though, via frank and sympathetic group conversations, they came to see that their habit—which had started as a way to kill time and socialize—had begun to consume their lives, harm their friendships, and spawn abusive behavior and regrettable sexual decisions. Over time, as the cravings of their addiction lessened, they began to feel, as one student put it, "strangely happy" (Berdik, 2014).

"It's cheered me up for some reason, I don't know why," reported one boy in the detox program. "I feel different. I can concentrate more." By the end of a full week of detox, students had reengaged with their friends and found time to rekindle forgotten interests, like reading books.

Unfortunately, when the program ended most reverted to their old ways, which wasn't abusing drugs or alcohol but rather engaging in an unhealthy, habitual relationship with their smartphones. Nonetheless, their so-called "digital detox" had given them a new ability to set aside their devices without FOMO (fear of missing out).

These teens are part of a growing trend in which people of all ages voluntarily unplug from the Internet and their smartphones for a few days to rebalance their digital and real lives. Many people find that cutting ties to the Web makes them feel less frenetic and more content. By tamping down their digital cravings, they're able to attend to deeper longings, including fostering more meaningful ties with others. The experience of traveling back to a simpler time (circa 2011) shows just how much smartphones and social media have changed our lives, likely rewired our brains, and altered how we interact with one another.

THE CURIOSITY CONNECTION

Sherry Turkle, who conducted numerous studies of the impact of technology on how we communicate, has found that young people—who often insist they have multitasking abilities adults lack and can, thus, move deftly between the real and digital worlds—poignantly acknowledge that, nonetheless, something is missing in their connections with others, starting with their own parents' divided attention as they futz with phones at dinner, the park, or school events.

Young people also report something missing in their real-life conversations with friends, which doesn't surprise Turkle, who can point to studies that show the mere presence of a phone on the table makes our conversations shallower; we tend to stick to lighter topics as we fear we'll get interrupted in the middle of heartfelt sharing. As a result, we're less likely to bare our souls, kick around big ideas, read others' emotions, or have the sorts of silences that provide openings to deeper issues, like our aspirations and values. When we "keep our phones in the landscape," Turkle observes, "we don't allow these conversations to happen" (Turkle, 2015).

RESTORING THE LOST ART OF QUIET CONVERSATION

Moreover, says Turkle, "When we communicate on our digital devices, we learn different habits . . . we start to expect faster answers. To get these, we ask one another simpler questions. We dumb down our communications, even on the most important matters." All of this tempts us, says Turkle, "to think that our little 'sips' of online connection add up to a big gulp of real conversation. But they don't" (Turkle, 2012).

In fact, it seems that some kids' excessive use of screen time may be depriving them of an essential skill: the ability to read one another's facial expressions, emotions, and nonverbal cues. At least, that's what we might glean from a study that invited 51 preteens to engage in a digital detox program by attending a five-day camp without their devices (Uhls et al., 2014); after less than a week, the preteens were better able than peers who had not attended the camp to infer emotional states from photographs of facial expressions and videos of people talking with the volume muted. So while the bad news may be that digital devices can reduce our ability to read one another's emotions, the good news may be that we can restore it fairly quickly after just a few days of unplugging from our smartphones and plugging into one another.

Kentucky teacher Paul Barnwell (2014) discovered as much when he spontaneously launched an unusual project with his high school class. After watching his students struggle to interview one another for an assignment, fumbling in their efforts to move beyond scripted questions and engage in spontaneous dialogue, he asked his students to put down the smartphones they'd been pecking away at furtively under their desks and announced that their next project would be to "practice a skill they all desperately needed: holding a conversation" (para. 2).

After a long, bewildered pause, one student finally raised his hand. "How is this going to work?"

As his students gradually came to appreciate—and improve—their conversational skills, Barnwell realized "that conversational competence may be the most overlooked skill we fail to teach our kids." Indeed, "in our zealous rush to meet 21st century demands—emailing assignments, customizing projects for tablets and laptops, and allowing students to BYOD (bring your own device)—we aren't asking students to think and communicate in real time."

CHOOSING FACE-TO-FACE OVER FACEBOOK

What these studies and observations may add up to is that, like the proverbial frogs in a boiling pot, our world has gradually—yet dramatically and irreversibly—changed around us in ways we've been slow to recognize. Like the tremendous changes at the turn of the 20th century, the turn of the 21st century has brought a whole new set of dramatic changes; increasingly, our world is filled with strangers and superficial interactions that have morphed into a hyperfrenetic society that our great-grandparents would scarcely recognize or know how to navigate.

We've learned to cope with these rapid changes by becoming bystanders in one another's lives, often substituting the occasional "like" or thumbs-up on social media for real human contact. These connections don't serve us well, though, as a recent review of dozens of studies comprising 35,000 people seems to suggest: Higher use of social media correlates with mental depression, especially if people spend much time at all comparing the selectively curated glimpses of other people's lives to their own (Baker & Algorta, 2016). And among teens, Twenge and her colleagues found that high use of social media was linked to mental depression and suicidal thoughts, especially for teens who report low levels of in-person interactions (Twenge et al., 2018).

"Americans in the twenty-first century devote more technology to staying connected than any society in history, yet somehow the devices fail us: Studies show that we feel increasingly alone," write Harvard Medical School psychologists Jaqueline Olds and Richard Schwartz (2009) in the opening lines of their book, *The Lonely American: Drifting Apart in the 21st Century*. Olds and Schwartz note that the number of people with whom Americans say they discuss "important matters" dropped from three to two confidants between 1985 and 2004; more poignantly, the percentage of Americans who say they have no one in whom to confide tripled, rising to a full quarter of those surveyed.

Moreover, in light of medical research showing that social connections help us to live longer, respond better to stress, and ward off illness, Olds and Schwartz (and others) note this epidemic of loneliness is also turning into a health crisis and speculate that the rising number of adults and adolescents who use antidepressants may be related (at least in part) to the lack of meaningful interpersonal connections in their lives. According to a meta-analysis of 148 studies involving more than 300,000 patients, the stress of chronic loneliness has the same negative effects on health outcomes as smoking 15 cigarettes a day (Holt-Lunstand et al., 2010).

BECOMING CURIOUS ABOUT ONE ANOTHER

As we'll see, one possible antidote to loneliness, detachment, and declining empathy in our world of strangers may well be *curiosity*, albeit a more heartfelt version of curiosity that's less fixated on what other people *do* or *like*—their vacations, kids' activities, or reposts of news stories—and more intent on getting to something deeper, something that may have emerged more naturally in tight-knit communities where having fewer, deeper, more-intimate connections with those familiar to us may have provided something more meaningful than our smartphones could ever offer.

At this point, we might wonder: Can we really develop deeper connections with others? After all, don't relationships develop slowly (if not serendipitously) over a long period of time? Moreover, what could curiosity possibly have to do with intimacy?

Sure, it might be easy to chalk up intimacy and interpersonal connections to the vicissitudes of attraction and chance encounters—and to write off meaningful interpersonal relationships as enigmatic phenomena unrelated to curiosity—were it not for two research psychologists falling in love more than four decades ago and deciding to spend their lives researching this funny little thing called love.

CURIOUS ABOUT LOVE

As Arthur and Elaine Aron tell it, one kiss changed their lives. It was the summer of love, 1967. Both were students at the University of California, Berkeley, standing in front of Dwinelle Hall. "I fell in love very intensely," Arthur Aron recalls (Anwar, 2015). Rather serendipitously, he was also looking for a topic for his doctoral dissertation, so "just for fun I looked for the research on love, but there was almost none." So it was that the topic for his dissertation and, eventually, his life's work, came to him out of the blue, almost like a song.

In the coming years, he and Elaine would work together to apply scientific methods to study the secrets to not only romantic love but also interpersonal closeness. Over the years, they developed and refined a list of 36 questions that they have asked thousands of randomly assigned pairs of strangers to respond to with one another to see what effect they have on drawing people together. Although it wasn't the intent of the study, at least one pair of strangers got married six months after participating in the experiment (Aron, 2015), which contributed to reports that the

36 questions can lead to love—including a 2015 article in *The New York Times* that went viral in which Mindy Len Catron (2015) recounted how, on a lark, she and a casual acquaintance took the 36 questions out for a spin and wound up standing on a bridge at midnight, staring into each other's eyes, and eventually (spoiler alert!) falling in love.

THIRTY-SIX QUESTIONS TO INTIMACY

So what are these 36 questions, and what do they tell us about how to develop true interpersonal connections? Moreover, given that the sessions lasted only about 45 minutes—roughly the time it takes for pizza delivery—how might we use them (or some portion of them) to help students restore the interpersonal connections that seem to have gotten lost in our superficial, frenetic, digital, and impersonal society? As it turns out, the 36 questions are grouped into three sets that foster increasingly intimate dialogue. The first set encourages participants to share their preferences and interesting things about one another with questions like these:

- Given the choice of anyone in the world, whom would you want as a dinner guest?

- Would you like to be famous? In what way?

- Take four minutes and tell your partner as much about your life story as possible.

The second set encourages conversation pairs to share their aspirations and values, revealing personal information about themselves, and to talk about each other in a positive way, with questions like these:

- Is there something that you've dreamed of doing for a long time? Why haven't you done it?

- What do you value most in a friendship?

- How do you feel about your relationship with your mother?

- Alternate sharing something you consider a positive characteristic of your partner. Share a total of five items.

The third and final set of questions invites participants to become more vulnerable with one another, revealing personal and emotional information by responding to questions like these:

- Complete this sentence: "I wish I had someone with whom I could share . . ."
- Share with your partner an embarrassing moment in your life.

Participants then share what they like about each other and find shared connections with prompts like these:

- Make three true "we" statements each. For instance, "We are both in this room, feeling . . ."
- Share a personal problem and ask your partner's advice on how to handle it. Ask your partner to reflect back to you how you seem to feel about the problem you have chosen.

Together, the 36 questions compress into less than an hour what might normally take people weeks, months, or even years to share, moving them well past skimming the surface of their personalities (i.e., their *preferences*) to diving into their *values, aspirations, emotions,* and *regrets* before fostering *shared appreciation* and *mutual dependency* as they solve each other's problems. In many ways, they turn a brief conversation into the essence of *community*— shared values, aspirations, and dependency.

Time and again, the Arons and their colleagues discovered that after just 45 minutes of responding to these questions, partners reported a much higher sense of interpersonal closeness with each other than people in control groups who engaged in unstructured small talk. Moreover, partners experienced the same effects regardless of whether they were paired randomly or intentionally based upon shared values or even *conflicting* values (Aron et al., 1997). In other words, talking about values, aspirations, regrets, and challenges brought people of all stripes together, perhaps because it revealed there is more that unites than divides us.

It's worth noting how different these conversations are from chit chat when smartphones are in the "landscape" or the unending stream of tweets, likes, and pins on social media. At best, we might only share our preferences as we cheer on (or lament) our favorite sports teams, share vacation photos, or brag about our kids, but we do little to convey deep emotions or values, develop mutual dependency, or help one another solve real problems—the sort of values-based bonds that formed the fabric of smaller communities of yore and are increasingly rare in today's larger, more impersonal societies.

What does any of this have to do with curiosity? Quite a lot, as one of Arthur Aron's students discovered while digging deeper into the question of what makes love grow—and fade.

12

FALLING IN LOVE WITH CURIOSITY

While working in Arthur Aron's research laboratory at Stony Brook University in New York, Todd Kashdan began to wonder what personality traits drive attraction in the first place. As with any set of data, the 36-question experiment produced variable results. Overall, the results were positive, but some conversation pairs formed even stronger bonds than others. Why should that be? Were some people more socially anxious than others, inhibiting their ability to connect? Did some people listen better? Were some people simply more positive, making them more likeable? Or could something else be at work . . . like *curiosity*?

Upon leaving Arthur Aron's lab for a position at the State University of New York at Buffalo, Kashdan began studying curiosity, exploring its links with such things as personal growth and goal attainment. Thinking back on his work with Arthur Aron, he wondered if curiosity might support *interpersonal connections*. Could curious people be better listeners, asking better follow-up questions and showing more interest in their conversation partners than incurious people? As no one had yet researched what role curiosity might play in forming interpersonal connections, Kashdan decided to follow his hunch and devised an experiment with his colleague, John Roberts (2004).

I LIKE YOU WHEN YOU'RE CURIOUS ABOUT ME

They invited 104 college students to engage in conversations with a stranger (in this case, a fellow student), following a simplified set of questions inspired by the Arons' 36 questions. Unbeknownst to the participants, their conversation partners were confederates of Kashdan and Roberts, trained to provide friendly yet neutral interactions during the conversations and report afterward on their experiences. Like the 36-questions experiment, the conversations began with small talk but soon became increasingly intimate, employing just five questions:

- If you could invite anyone, living or dead, for dinner and conversation, who would it be and why?

- Is there anything you find disturbing about immortality? If not, why not?

- If a crystal ball would tell you the truth about any one thing you wished to know concerning yourself, life, the future, or anything else, what would you want to know?

- Is there something that you've dreamed of doing for a long time? Why haven't you done it?

- When did you last cry in front of another person? By yourself?

Prior to the study, Kashdan and Roberts had measured participants on three scales:

1. Their general and current levels of social anxiety (how confident or fearful they felt in social situations and going into the experiment)

2. Their positive and negative affect (for example, whether such conversations made them feel joyful and excited versus anxious and jittery)

3. Their levels of *trait* and *state* curiosity (how curious they felt in general and during the study)

Afterward, Kashdan and Roberts measured participants' interpersonal attraction and perceived closeness—the extent, for example, they believed they could "get along" or would "like to work together" with their conversation partners. As a result, they now had several data points to compare using sophisticated statistical methods. Upon crunching the numbers, some surprises emerged.

First, participants with higher levels of *state* curiosity (and to a lesser extent, *trait* curiosity) reported feeling closer to their conversation partners afterward. Perhaps most strikingly, though, so did their conversation partners—who, recall, were confederates instructed to remain friendly yet consistently even-keeled with their conversation partners. Interestingly, positive affect had *no correlation* with interpersonal closeness for participants or confederates—that is, enjoying the conversations didn't help participants feel closer to their partners if their partners weren't also *curious* about them.

TURNING SMALL TALK INTO DIALOGUE

In subsequent experiments, Kashdan found that curious people appear to have a natural knack for turning small talk into deeper, more meaningful conversations. For example, he and his colleagues invited participants (whom they pretested and identified as having varying levels of trait curiosity) to engage in 45-minute conversations with strangers—with half of the conversations designed to be superficial banter, answering questions like "What is your favorite holiday? Why?" and the other half designed to be more intimate conversations with prompts like "When did you last cry in front of another person? By yourself?" (Kashdan et al., 2011).

Not surprisingly, participants who engaged in the intimate conversations reported greater feelings of intimacy with their conversation partners than those who engaged in small talk. Yet some small-talk conversation pairs stood out as outliers, reporting feelings of closeness on par with those engaged in the conversations structured for intimacy. What turned the small talk into more intimate conversation? As you might've guessed, at least one member of the pair was highly *curious*. From these findings, we might extrapolate that when we're curious—and in the presence of someone curious—even relatively brief small-talk conversations can turn into something more meaningful.

So what exactly were curious people doing to turn small talk into meaningful conversations? For privacy reasons, Kashdan didn't record or make transcripts of the conversations, yet he found that people who were highly curious were deemed by their partners to be more open, tolerant, and energetic than noncurious people. Curious people seem to enter into dialogue with open minds and an eagerness to learn about someone else, which in turn encourages others to open up to them. That's the symbiosis between curiosity and intimacy; curious people delight in learning something new, and their conversation partners delight in having someone understand them.

At first blush, that may seem like an asymmetrical sort of symbiosis—with one person satisfying an *intellectual* need (curiosity) and the other an *emotional* one (closeness). That hardly seems empathetic—after all, isn't the best way to connect with someone to assure them that we "feel their pain"?

Well, perhaps not.

THE PERILS OF FEELING YOUR PAIN

As it turns out, we human beings have an amazing capacity to *literally* feel someone else's pain; numerous experiments have shown that when we see someone else experiencing pain, it fires the same regions of our brains as are fired when we ourselves experience the same pain (Singer & Klimecki, 2014). In fact, we have so much ability to experience another's pain that we're subject to emotional contagion, "catching" others' emotional states and internalizing them as our own. That's great when they're experiencing joy or enthusiasm—or when it propels us to rush to another's aid. But it can drag us down when others are feeling rage, pain, deep sadness, or hopelessness, which can create something researchers call *empathic distress*—or in layperson's terms, *burnout*.

To insulate ourselves from feeling too much pain or negative emotion, we may withdraw from others. Studies have found that the longer students are in medical school, for example, the less empathy they demonstrate—with the greatest declines occurring as they begin working with real patients who are suffering and dying (Neumann et al., 2011).

One way that people tend to insulate themselves from empathic pain is to view the person in pain as a member of a different group than ourselves. The same brain scans that show we can feel someone else's pain also show that we tend to suppress our empathic responses when the person in pain is a member of an out-group (e.g., a player on a different team) or someone we think deserved their pain (e.g., we thought the other player was cheating during the game; Singer & Klimecki, 2014).

Interpersonal curiosity works against both impulses. It does something else that's vitally important and requires that we understand the difference between *empathy* and *compassion*, at least in psychological terms. Empathy is *feeling with* another person, while compassion is *feeling for* them—that is, being concerned for their well-being and wanting to help them, yet not necessarily mirroring or internalizing their emotions. Researchers sometimes express this distinction as *cognitive* versus *affective* empathy. When we experience cognitive empathy, we appreciate another's needs while maintaining sufficient emotional distance to serve as an objective partner in helping them solve their problems; when we experience affective empathy, we're more apt to get sucked into feeling another's emotions and pain, which ultimately can lead to distress, clouded judgment, and the need to withdraw from them. Brain scans, in fact, show that we activate different parts of our brains when we feel empathy versus compassion (Singer & Klimecki, 2014).

Studies have found, in fact, that we're more likely to help someone when we feel compassion for them versus experiencing empathic distress (Batson, 2009). Perhaps even more important, compassion isn't simply a personality trait. Indeed, it's possible to *train* people to become more compassionate by engaging in what's called "loving kindness training," which often includes silent, meditative exercises in which participants visualize a person they feel close to and generate feelings of kindness toward them. Over time, they learn to transfer these feelings of kindness toward others, including strangers and people with whom they have difficulties. After such training, participants are happier and more likely to engage in altruistic behaviors (Fredericksen et al., 2008).

So how can we use curiosity to foster better relationships? Here are a few musings to ponder.

Musing #1: Put Down Our Phones and Just Talk

Let's start by not fooling ourselves into thinking that we're meaningfully connecting with others through social media. Sure, it can be a fun way to share photos and track down long-lost cousins, but for conversations that really matter, our tweets, texts, and posts aren't the stuff of true connection. If anything, they may just get in the way because we can find it easier to post something inflammatory on social media that we'd never say at a dinner party.

At home, you can create "off hours" for your phones or try a "digital detox" on your next family vacation. A few years ago, my family did precisely that on a road trip to New Mexico. We all left our phones at home or packed them away to be looked at only once a day for a specified half-hour block of time. I only brought mine for directions, leaving it in the car when we arrived at our destination. Initially, we all experienced some symptoms of withdrawal. For example, for the first day or two I'd often feel a phantom phone vibrate in my empty pocket. After a few days, though, we all felt more at ease. My out-of-office reply for work emails worked just fine—my brief check-ins during our daily 30-minute digital sneak-a-peeks convinced me that the rest of the world was getting along just fine without me.

At night, sitting beneath Southwestern sunsets, our conversations were deep and rich, touching on many of the topics raised in the Arons' 36 questions (though I didn't even know about them at the time). My daughters shared their aspirations for school, life, love, and happiness. And they asked my wife and me questions—about how we met, fell in love, and were drawn to our chosen professions. With no phones in the landscape to interrupt us, we fell into a nightly tradition of selecting one member of the family and taking turns sharing what we most admired about them. Often, we'd look around the restaurant and feel sorry for other people sitting around us, noses buried in their phones, dining alone together.

Musing #2: Ask One Question a Day That Goes Beyond the Superficial

Now that our phones are out of the way, let's really talk, going beyond the superficial and finding out what makes other people tick—their experiences, values, and aspirations. Here's one simple way to take a conversation to a deeper level: Add two little words—*for you*—to any question. It works like this: What was the best moment of your family vacation—*for you*? What's the best part of your job—*for you*? What will be the most difficult aspect of this task—*for you*?

Tacking these two simple words onto a question—and giving adequate wait time—does two things. First, it helps people consider their own emotions, needs, and challenges. I've found sometimes it can create a sort of confessional experience; people will admit that maybe they're being too hasty, judgmental, or leery of conflict. Second, those two little words show others you care enough to find out what's in their hearts and on their minds—in short, you're curious about them.

Sure, it may feel more comfortable to chat about the weather, sports, or each other's jobs, but if we want to feel real connections with others, we can start by wondering what they *value, aspire to*, or *feel*. And we can use those two little words—*for you*—to draw those things out of them.

Musing #3: Appreciate Each Other

Years ago, when Stephen Covey identified the habits of highly effective people, he called out their ability to "seek first to understand, then be understood" (Covey, 1989). In many ways, that statement captures what it means to be curious about others, although true interpersonal curiosity likely goes a step further, seeking first to *appreciate* others—that is, not only understanding how someone feels but also valuing their perspectives and having their best interests at heart.

In other words, true interpersonal curiosity appreciates another person's experiences, perspectives, values, and aspirations—and feels kindness toward them. (After all, psychopaths and con artists are adept at *understanding* others—and using that knowledge to manipulate them). We don't have to agree with others, mind you; we may disagree, yet we can still appreciate how their experiences and emotions could lead them to a different perspective than ours, even as we resist the urge to cast them into an outgroup and judge them.

The good news is that curiosity is innate in all of us, so we never fully lose our interpersonal curiosity—even though we may at times become too distracted, disconnected, or frenetic to slow down and listen to what others want to tell us. Deep down, we're all curious; we like learning about other people and what makes them tick. Also, we're social creatures. We crave connecting with others in meaningful ways. Connecting those two dots—our need for connection and our innate curiosity—need not be complicated or difficult. That's not to say it's easy, either.

So let's really appreciate each other (and help students appreciate one another)—recognizing one another's *full worth*. We can start by removing empathy killers in our own thinking—including labeling someone as a member of an out-group or a perpetrator of her or his own suffering. True, people often make bad decisions that lead to their unhappiness. We all make mistakes. Once we get past that, we're better able to appreciate that no one is a "flat character"—we all have backstories that influence who we become, what we value, and where we want to go with our lives. As the adage goes, we all have at least one book inside us. Curiosity can help us to find—and appreciate—what those stories might be.

CONNECTING WITH CURIOSITY

The tragic murder of Kitty Genovese more than 50 years ago—and the seeming callousness of bystanders—sparked much soul searching about the decline of compassion in our increasingly urban society and led to academic inquiry into the bystander effect. An important detail omitted from the original telling of the story was that one neighbor, Sophia Farrar, had risked her own life to rush to aid Kitty, cradling her in her arms as she died. The subsequent narrative that modern society had turned all of us into callous human beings with no connection, concern, or regard for one another was never quite true.

Nonetheless, the story struck a chord—likely stoking a reasonable fear that if we're not curious about one another, we *could* lose something as we transition from small communities to larger urban (and now digital) societies. Moreover, we probably shouldn't be too quick to romanticize those tight-knit communities of yore; they could also be stifling, oppressive places where values were more often imposed than shared—as a great deal of literature ought to remind us, including Nathaniel Hawthorne's *The Scarlet Letter*, Maya Angelou's *I Know Why the Caged Bird Sings*, Harper Lee's *To Kill a Mockingbird*, and Arthur Miller's *The Crucible*—to name but a few examples.

What interpersonal curiosity might allow us to do, though, is not necessarily go back to those places of imposed values and conformity, but instead help us discover new shared values and connections, shifting our focus from solely what other people *do* that gives them value to consider instead what they feel, believe, and share with us.

Many writers, including *The New York Times* columnist Barbara Ehrenreich (1985), have lamented our modern "cult of conspicuous busyness." We define ourselves by what makes us busy—our jobs, our kids' activities, and our accomplishments. What gets lost in our frenetic busyness may be the deeper conversations we all need to feel less lonely and more connected—the very conversations that provide the opportunity to share our values and aspirations. As we'll see in the final section of this book, it's connections with others that often serve as the source of true well-being and happiness. As obvious as this sounds, it's a lesson that many people learn too late—or never at all.

A TOOL KIT FOR ENCOURAGING INTERPERSONAL CURIOSITY

A key element of social-emotional learning is learning to be curious about other people's feelings, experiences, and perspectives. Yet school personnel already have a lot on their plates and may bristle at the prospect of needing to add yet another new "program" to their plates to address a large societal concern. So the following tools are designed to be embedded in student learning experiences, starting with unplugging from their phones and studying the results.

Tool 7: Encourage a "Disconnect Challenge"

Key idea: Inviting students to take a voluntary break from smartphones and social media can help them see the impact both have on their lives and their relationships.

Many schools and teachers—often as part of a psychology, study skills, or science class—have invited students to voluntarily study the effects of spending a few days without their phones and social media. Typically, students find the experiences, while difficult at first, to be eye-opening and even transformative. Here's how many schools create these experiences.

1. Gather and share with students the research on smartphones and mental health. You might share information from this book and other articles about the link between smartphone and social media use and mental health as well as anecdotes from students who "survived" the challenge and experienced a surge in contentment and well-being.

2. Invite students into the challenge (and to play a leadership role). To generate buy-in, make the challenge voluntary and, ideally, student-led.

3. Before you start, encourage students to take an honest self-assessment. Help students collect before-and-after data. Many apps, for example, track time spent on phones and social media. Encourage students to collect these baseline data along with a few simple indicators of their well-being (e.g., rating how much they agree with statements like "It feels good to be alive," "I enjoy life as much as anyone," or "I've had meaningful conversations with family and friends in the past 24 hours").

4. Set a limited period (e.g., five days, one week) and "rules" for the detox. Because it's easier to contemplate going "cold turkey" for a short period of time, limit the challenge to just a few days or a week. Also, create some shared "rules" for acceptable use of phones (e.g., calling parents or places of employment).

5. Invite students to reflect on and share how they feel during the detox. They can do this with journal writing, video journals, or in person with one another. In fact, it's important to frame the "detox" as a shared experience. Help them reflect on the arc of their emotions and behaviors. Do they experience FOMO (fear of missing out)? Does the fear subside? Do they have different conversations with friends and family? Do they have more time to read and reflect? Do they feel bored? More creative? More content?

6. At the end of the challenge, invite students to reassess how they feel. Tracking pre- and post-data will help students see some important changes in their well-being.

7. Afterward, invite them to set new personal goals for managing their digital lives. The aim isn't for students to trade in their smartphones for carrier pigeons, but to consider how to better balance their personal and digital lives. Encourage them to set goals—perhaps even using apps to track smartphone use and/or curb their addictions.

Tool 8: Embed Perspective Taking Into Learning

Key idea: Seeking to understand and appreciate others' experiences and way of thinking (i.e., having interpersonal curiosity) is an important social-emotional (and critical thinking) skill.

It's possible for students of all ages to consider other people's perspectives and feelings. Here are some ways to engage students in perspective taking—an important social-emotional learning skill linked to compassion and critical thinking:

- Encourage students to peel back the layers. We can help students of all ages understand that people's actions are driven by their feelings and past experiences. So as you're reading a text or discussing a character's or person's actions, invite students to consider that character's *feelings* and *motives* (e.g., Why is Roscuro the rat so bitter?). Older students can engage in more complex thinking, dissecting circumstances or prior experiences that influence people's attitudes or behaviors (e.g., Why do you think Mama and Walter Lee Younger have such different views on how to spend the insurance money?). Basically, you're asking students to dig more deeply to appreciate how people's experiences can lead them to view the same events or opportunities quite differently.

- Invite *possibilities*. You can encourage students to consider a variety of perspectives by reframing questions that seem to have a single answer (e.g., Why did Tories in the American colonies support the British?) to more open-ended questions (e.g., What are some possible reasons many colonists chose to remain loyal to the crown?) and invite multiple students to respond to the question. You can use this simple technique in a variety of subject areas—inviting students to offer different approaches to solving math problems, explaining science phenomena, or interpreting a literary character's motives.

- View images in the eyes of different beholders. Invite students to closely observe an image (e.g., a historic photograph or painting related to a topic they're learning) that can be interpreted in different ways and invite them (silently at first) to record their observations. Next, invite them to share (in a small or whole-class group) what they noticed. Note differences in the observations and engage students in a dialogue about the differences, including why there's not necessarily a "right" or "wrong" way to view the image and how other people's perspectives help us see the world in richer, deeper ways.

- Walk a mile in another's shoes. This phrase (from *To Kill a Mockingbird*) is the essence of interpersonal curiosity. It encourages students to consider (i.e., become *curious* about) others' experiences, and those experiences shape their beliefs, aspirations, actions, and opinions (e.g., What is Chief Joseph feeling as he surrenders to General Howard?). Second, you can help them appreciate those differences by imagining themselves in the same circumstances as the character, person, or writer (e.g., What would you have done if you were Rosa Parks? Would you have given up your seat?).

- Create a "flipped" narrative. After reading a parody or rewrites of popular fiction, such as *The True Story of the Three Little Pigs* by Jon Scieszka (which tells the story from the wolf's perspective) or *Wicked: The Life and Times of the Wicked Witch of the West* (which rewrites *The Wizard of Oz* from the witch's perspective), you can invite students to do the same with other popular fables, movies, or stories—contemplating how, in keeping with the adage that we all believe ourselves to be the protagonist in our life story, an antagonist might be misunderstood or a victim of circumstances.

Tool 9: Help Students Listen With Curious Compassion

Key idea: We can help students develop curious compassion by teaching them how to engage in active listening.

As Paul Barnwell discovered in his classroom, many students have yet to learn the art of conversation. Here are some strategies you can teach students, drawn from the counseling strategy of "active listening" and studies of interpersonal curiosity, to help them engage in deep conversation:

- Just listen. Don't think about what you'll say next. Listen to what other people are saying, considering what emotions they're feeling and perspectives they're sharing.

- Show others you're listening. Make eye contact. Lean in. Nod. Offer feedback that mirrors their emotions (e.g., "That must've been exciting/frustrating/frightening").

- Let the other person talk. Don't interject new ideas or redirect the conversation to yourself (e.g., "That reminds me of a time that I . . .").

- Stay curious. Don't pass judgment—or rush to solutions. Just listen and do your best to understand and appreciate their perspective—to see the world from their point of view.

- When it's your turn to talk, first ask questions to gain deeper understanding. These include questions about, for example, your conversation partners' feelings (e.g., "How do you feel about what happened?") and aspirations (e.g., "What do you hope will happen?").

- Provide affirmation. Talk about others in a positive way—one that shows them you understand and appreciate them (e.g., "I can tell you really have a heart for others").

- Connect with shared experiences and values. Highlight something you have in common with your conversation partners related to what they've just shared (e.g., "I feel the same way about that" or "I can really relate to what you're saying").

EL Schools: Embedding Empathy Into the Curriculum

Across 150-plus EL (formerly known as Expeditionary Learning) schools nationwide, students develop compassionate curiosity not just as a side program or one-time student assembly but rather through the regular curriculum that teaches them how to be good listeners, consider other perspectives, and empathize with others' experiences while studying and discussing literature. It starts with a curriculum development team that thoughtfully selects and integrates fiction and nonfiction texts into a unit—for example, reading the novel *Esperanza Rising*, a historical fiction

(*Continued*)

(Continued)

novel that describes the challenges of a Mexican immigrant family, while also reading the *Universal Declaration of Human Rights* so they could view Esperanza's experiences through the lens of human rights.

"We begin with the four *T*s of instruction: topic, task, target, text," EL's chief curriculum developer, Christina Riley, explained (Stringer, 2019). They identify *topics* that will arouse students' compassion and curiosity, select *texts* to elucidate the topic, develop challenging performance *tasks* that ensure students meet learning *targets*—including both academic standards (e.g., analyzing literature) and social-emotional skills (e.g., self-regulation and compassion). For example, as they read, teachers might ask students, "What happened with a character there—he exploded in a fit of rage. Did that get him what he wanted or needed?" (Stringer, 2019). On their final performance tasks, students typically draw connections between what they're learning and their own lives.

The usual sequence for this learning, according to Riley, is "read, think, talk, write." Students read a text, think about it, discuss it with peers, then write to reflect on its meaning. EL teachers don't leave student discussion to chance, though—rather, they scaffold students' dialogue by providing sentence starters (e.g., Can you tell me more about that? I would like to respectfully disagree with you.). Afterward, they invite students to reflect on how their conversations went.

On top of that, they teach directly the kinds of behaviors and dispositions they want students to develop. "It's really hard for students to understand what empathy is," notes Riley. So teachers engage students in conversations about what it means, for example, to feel empathy and then, with students, create posters to hang on classroom walls that fully describe the character traits that they want students to develop. "Otherwise, it's just a very abstract term."

So what are the biggest obstacles to encouraging compassionate curiosity among students? Time and leadership, says Riley. Focusing on teaching interpersonal curiosity and compassion consistently yields significant, positive changes in classroom and school culture, but it's often the first thing teachers drop from the curriculum when they feel pressed for time. When leaders prioritize teaching empathy and compassion, it tends to stick. When they don't, it tends to face elimination. In short, for curiosity, compassion, perspective taking, and active listening to happen at the classroom level, it requires a schoolwide focus.

PART V

CURIOUS FOR GOOD

Among the most important capacities that you take with you today is your curiosity. You must guard it, for curiosity is the beginning of empathy.

—Dr. Atul Gawande

13

THE SEARCH FOR HAPPINESS

In late April 1991, Chris McCandless ventured alone into the Alaskan wilderness near Denali National Park on a quest to disconnect from society, be one with nature, and find deeper meaning in his life. For two years, since graduating from Emory University, he'd been on a curiosity-fueled odyssey. After ditching his car in the Arizona desert, he turned his back on his family, wealth, and privilege and went off the grid as he hitchhiked and hopped freight trains across the American West. He lived with vagrants in Arizona, slept in a homeless shelter in Los Angeles, worked on farms in South Dakota, and kayaked down the Colorado River into the Gulf of California, where he spent 36 days living off a five-pound bag of rice and whatever he could catch in the sea.

From what his biographer, Jon Krakauer (1996), could glean from McCandless's journal, the young man hoped for Alaska to be his "final and greatest adventure"—where, "no longer poisoned by . . . civilization" he would "kill the false being within and victoriously conclude the spiritual revolution." After more than two months living off the land—hunting, fishing, and eating berries and other plants—he came to an epiphany while reading Leo Tolstoy's novella *Family Happiness* and underlined these words in the crumpled paperback book he'd carried into the wild:

> He was right in saying that the only certain happiness in life is to live for others. I have lived through much and now think I have found what is needed for happiness. A quiet life in the country, with the possibility of being useful to people

to whom it is easy to do good then work which one hopes may be of some use; then rest, nature, books, music, love for one's neighbor—such is my idea of happiness.

After living for many weeks in complete isolation, Tolstoy's words jumped off the page for McCandless, giving him a profound insight: The key to happiness is *living for others*. The next day, July 3, he patched his jeans, shaved for the first time in months, photographed himself for posterity, packed his gear, and prepared to hike 20 miles back to civilization, concluding a long spiritual journey and rejoining humanity.

Tragically, he would never again see another person. The wilderness in which he had sought refuge seemingly turned on him, barring his return (the exact causes are unknown; perhaps illness or flooded rivers). He died alone, in an abandoned bus deep in the woods, miles from another soul.

On one hand, we might view Chris's tragic fate as a cautionary tale of the perils of unrestrained youthful curiosity. Yet McCandless's intellectual and physical explorations helped him compress what others take a lifetime to learn (and many may never learn)—that only after we stop chasing pleasure and begin to appreciate the beauty around us and connect deeply with others can we find meaning and purpose in our lives. As we'll see, it's often when we reframe our pursuit of happiness that we achieve a sort of quiet contentment and sense of well-being.

RED, WHITE, AND THE BLUES

Although the immoderate nature of McCandless's wanderings may have been unusual, what sparked it—an apparent gnawing emptiness inside—is hardly unique. Many Americans, despite having what in global terms amounts to staggering wealth, appear to be searching in vain for happiness. For example, among 34 developed nations, Americans' happiness fell from third to 19th over the past 10 years (Sachs, 2017). And on a worldwide survey that asked some 130,000 people in 130 nations if they had experienced positive emotions the day before (e.g., "Did you smile or laugh a lot yesterday?"), Americans fell squarely in the middle of the pack, behind people from impoverished places like Guatemala (Gallup, 2017).

Of course, overall increases in American's average per capita income mask the reality that, since the 1980s, only a small percentage of wealthy people have experienced substantial gains in personal income; meanwhile, wages and wealth for the rest of Americans have stagnated or declined. Indeed, while the US remains the world's wealthiest nation, it's also its most inequitable in terms of both income and wealth. According to a report from retirement and financial services firm Allianz, on a scale of 0 to 100, with 0 being perfect equality and 100 being one person controlling all the wealth, the US has a score of 80.6—the fourth highest, putting us in the dubious company of Turkey, Mexico, and Chile (Sherman, 2015).

So it's entirely possible that a widening gulf between the haves and have-nots may be behind reported declines in American happiness—after all, psychologists have long observed that people feel happy when they believe they are keeping—up with, if not outpacing, the Joneses. In simple terms, we feel happier when we perceive ourselves as better off than our family, friends, and neighbors and, conversely, less happy if we see others in our immediate circles faring better than us—a phenomenon that's exacerbated nowadays by social media, television reality programs, and advertising that makes us feel everyone else is better off than we are—from celebrities to friends to former classmates ("How does *that guy* have a boat?"). As a result, we may feel those income gaps even more acutely and fall into a sort of collective funk.

Research, however, suggests another explanation for why America seems to remain so far from being the world's most satisfied nation. Among people in wealthier nations, in particular, income becomes less predictive of life satisfaction. Beyond a certain point, incremental increases in personal wealth do not correspond with continued increases in happiness; after a point, gains in wealth often correlate with *declines* in happiness. Basically, wealth and happiness are correlated in a curvilinear fashion—a sort of inverted U—with increases in wealth correlating with increases in happiness as people move out of poverty, a leveling off at middle-income levels, and a downward bend at higher-income levels (Diener & Biswas-Diener, 2002). In fact, after a point (an annual income of about $75,000 per year; Kahneman & Deaton, 2010) rising income becomes less important and even averse to happiness as it's linked with higher divorce rates, greater stress, and less time to enjoy the good things in life. As the researchers who synthesized these studies put it bluntly, "Our advice is to avoid poverty, live in a rich country, and focus on goals other than material wealth" (Diener & Biswas-Diener, 2002, p. 161).

So if material wealth (at least after a point) isn't the key to happiness, what is? To answer this question, we need to understand the nature of happiness itself and how it comes to us in different forms, which, interestingly, reflects what we know about curiosity and its different forms.

DIFFERENT TYPES OF HAPPINESS

As far back as Aristotle, philosophers have observed that happiness is not a single state of being, but many. For starters, there's *hedonic* happiness—sometimes known as pleasures of the flesh (e.g., eating, drinking, thrill seeking, and other delights). The trouble with this form of happiness, as philosophers and researchers alike have noted, is that it tends to wane over time—it has diminishing returns. That has a lot to do with our brain chemicals; pleasure is associated with quick hits of dopamine, which fade quickly, like neurochemical flash floods. As a result, we tend to experience diminishing returns with hedonic happiness as the novelty and the "buzz" of new experiences wears off, which leaves us seeking evergreater thrills to receive the same dopamine hit (Ryan & Deci, 2001). Sadly, many people never seem to move past seeking only this form of happiness and wind up on what researchers and therapists refer to as a "hedonic treadmill" (McMahan & Estes, 2011).

According to research, a deeper, more sustainable happiness can be found in *engagement*—in getting better at something that matters to us, be it a hobby, profession, or other pursuit. A large body of research, in fact, shows a strong link between achieving goals and well-being—one that's consistent across cultures, regardless of whether they are predominately individualistic or collectivistic (Ryan & Deci, 2001). Finally, and perhaps most importantly, well-being relates strongly to what Aristotle called *eudaemonia*—cultivating one's own virtues for the greater good. In simple terms, it's finding meaning or purpose to our lives by helping others (Peterson et al., 2007).

At this point, we might ask, If we know so much about happiness, why are so many people so miserable? For starters, it's likely that consuming a constant stream of advertising and other media, as many of us do, creates insatiable cravings, which we cannot satisfy—be it tropical resorts, luxury cars, beautiful skin, or flat abs. We're constantly exposed to what we *don't* have (and will probably never get), which leaves us spinning on hedonic hamster wheels, never feeling satisfied or attaining a deeper sense of well-being.

So what could help us step off the hedonic treadmill and find *real* happiness?

If we look to people who find real happiness—who report being uncommonly happy—we find they haven't followed common wisdom about *how* to be happy. They're not richer, sexier, or luckier. Rather, they've cultivated something many others lack. What is it? As you might have guessed, it's once again, *curiosity*—though a deeper, more reflective, and perhaps wiser form than what we've explored in previous chapters.

DOES CURIOSITY LEAD TO HAPPINESS . . . OR MISERY?

Let's start with the basics. We know from research that curiosity can spark little moments of delight that make life more enjoyable. One study found, for example, that people enjoyed listening to music more when they had no foreknowledge of what song they were about to hear next—that is, when each new (yet familiar) song came with a dose of anticipation—versus when they were told beforehand what song was coming next on a playlist (Hsee et al., 2015). This may explain why many of us prefer to listen to music in "shuffle" or "random-play" mode.

By the same token, curiosity can rob us of our happiness by compelling us, against our better judgment, to seek information that causes us distress. If, for example, we're told someone has posted something negative about us on social media, learning *exactly* what they posted won't do us much good; it will only stir negative emotions. Yet that's often exactly what many people do.

Studies in laboratory settings have found that people, in fact, tend to follow their curiosity to the detriment of their well-being. Researchers Christopher Hsee and Bowen Ruan, for example, found they could coax people into listening to the sound of nails on a chalkboard or looking at gross pictures of dog poop (boys will be boys, it seems) by creating a bit of mystery about which squares on a computer screen would yield a bland sound (water pouring into a glass) or innocuous image (of a stone) versus the distressing sound or revolting image. Study subjects could've clicked on none of the squares at all, yet when they were presented with "mystery squares," they couldn't help but to click on them (Hsee & Ruan, 2015). In a subsequent study, Hsee and Ruan (2016) went a step further to see if people would touch electrified pens sitting on a table out of mere curiosity to see which ones would shock them. They did. From these experiments, Hsee and Ruan concluded that curiosity may not *always* be good for us.

Of course, these were rather superficial experiments. Seeing a picture of dog poop or getting zapped by a pen won't leave you emotionally scarred for life; nor will listening to music on random play fill your life with meaning. What we really want to know is whether, in *real life,* curiosity makes us happy, turning every day into an adventure, helping us uncover new opportunities, meet new friends, and discover new interests. Or does it make us miserable, revealing the ugly truth about the world around us, rendering nothing sacred, and sending us into a downward spiral of stinking thinking, existential angst, and Ingmar Bergman films?

From a scientific perspective, these are difficult questions to answer with precision—after all, there's no curiosity pill to offer one group while slipping another a placebo. Yet as we'll see, if we knit together findings from several studies into a larger tapestry, a portrait begins to emerge for how curiosity can contribute to a life well lived—a life less about thrills, excitement, and giddiness and grounded instead in a deeper sense of satisfaction, well-being, and contentment.

CURIOUSLY HAPPY

A few years after discovering the power of curiosity in creating better relationships, Todd Kashdan teamed up with Michael Steger, who had been studying how people find meaning in their lives. Steger (2010) had observed that instead of filling their lives with good things—"good feelings, good relationships, good desires, good vacations, good purchasing decisions, good plans for the future, good sex, good health, good looks"—happy people accept that bad things are bound to happen from time to time and learn from them, using them as a springboard to achieving deeper insights and meaning in their lives. So in a sort of chocolate-mixing-with-peanut-butter experiment, the two researchers teamed up to explore whether *curious* people are happier in life.

GIVE ME A *C*: WHAT HAPPENS WHEN STUDENTS ARE CURIOUS

As both researchers were professors, they turned to a readily available population to study: college students, rounding up and surveying 97 of them on a variety of measures, including their *trait curiosity* (e.g., "I would describe myself as someone who actively seeks as much information as I can in a new situation"), *meaning and sense of life purpose* (e.g., "'I have a good sense of what makes my life meaningful"), positive and negative *outlook on life*, their *personality traits* (extraversion, neuroticism, openness to experience, agreeableness, and conscientiousness), and *overall life satisfaction* (e.g., "In most ways, my life is close to the ideal"; Kashdan & Steger, 2007). For 21 days, they tracked students' daily happiness and curiosity by asking them to track how *curious* they felt (e.g., "Everywhere I went, I was out looking for new things and experiences" and "When I was participating in activities, I got so involved that I lost track of time"), how much they engaged in *growth-oriented behaviors* (e.g., I "persevered at a valued goal even in the face of obstacles" or "expressed my gratitude for something someone did for me either verbally or in writing"), the extent to which they engaged in *hedonistic behaviors* (e.g., I "kept eating more than I intended of something just because it tasted so good" and I "had sex purely to get pleasure"), and finally, their sense of *life meaning* (e.g., "How meaningful does your life feel?" and "How much were you looking to find your life's purpose?").

An interesting pattern emerged in students' daily tallies of their curiosity and happiness. On days when they felt more *curious,* they reported more persistence, goal directedness, and greater life satisfaction and meaning. The daily logs also revealed that students with more trait curiosity found less pleasure in hedonic events than students with less trait curiosity. Although they still engaged in hedonistic behaviors (they were in college, after all), such activities were less apt to be the source of their happiness.

Less curious students, in contrast, were *only* happy on days when they experienced hedonic pleasure. Overall, they also experienced less life satisfaction and life meaning. Curious students, on the other hand, experienced satisfaction even on days when hedonic "pleasure" passed them by; in short, they appeared to find joy in everyday intellectual exploration and the search for meaning. These findings led Kashdan and Steger (2007) to conclude that "curiosity is an important, neglected process in the pursuit of a life well lived."

"RECHARGING" WITH CURIOSITY

Years later, researchers in Spain conducted a similar, weeklong study of 209 college students and discovered that curiosity put an extra spring in their steps, recharging their batteries. Every afternoon over a five-day period, students responded to measures in these areas:

- *Life meaning* ("Today, my life has a clear sense of purpose," and "Today, I was searching for something that made my life feel significant.")

- *State curiosity* ("Today, I found myself looking for new opportunities to grow as a person," or "Today, I became so involved in an activity that I lost track of time.")

- *Emotional state* ("At this moment, I feel happy," or "At this moment, I feel nervous.")

Later, in the evening, students reported how engaged they felt with their studies (e.g., "At my studies, I feel strong and vigorous") and their energy levels (e.g., "At this moment, I feel emotionally drained from my studies"). Comparing these two data points revealed that the more curious students felt in the afternoon, the less exhausted they felt in the evening (Garrosa et al., 2016). Curiosity seemed to energize them and help them sustain the sort of self-improvement and search for meaning that other studies suggest lie at the heart of life satisfaction.

THE LINK BETWEEN CURIOSITY AND LIFE SATISFACTION

Some large-scale studies suggest as much—that curiosity is linked to overall happiness in life. One such study mapped the results from more than 12,000 US adults taking a scientifically validated survey of 24 personality traits (the VIA survey) onto results from a second survey of life satisfaction and happiness in all three forms: hedonism, engagement, and meaning (Peterson et al., 2007). By comparing the results of these two surveys, the researchers could identify which personality traits were most strongly linked to people's life satisfaction. Here they are, listed in rank order:

- Zest (approaching experiences with excitement and energy)

- Hope (expecting the best in the future and working to achieve it)

- Love (valuing close relations with others)

- Gratitude (being aware of and thankful for the good things that happen)

- Curiosity (taking an interest in ongoing experience for its own sake)

Interestingly, curiosity ranked near the top of the list for all three types of happiness (seventh for *pleasure*, second for *engagement*, and fifth for *meaning*), which isn't all that surprising. After all, when we're curious, we're likely to seek new experiences, which can support hedonic pleasure—for example, we might discover a new favorite restaurant, band, or weekend pastime. Also, as we've seen, when we're curious we're more apt to cultivate and pursue personal interests, which supports engagement. Finally, when we're curious, we're more apt to discover deeper life purpose and meaning.

DOES CURIOSITY CHASE AWAY THE BLUES?

A similar but smaller study in Poland points to the intriguing possibility that curiosity may serve to keep the blues at bay (Kaczmarek et al., 2014). Researchers surveyed 257 people from ages 18 to 64 on measures of two types of curiosity: *stretching* ("Everywhere I go, I am out looking for new things or experiences") and *embracing* ("I am the type of person who really enjoys the uncertainty of everyday life") and compared their responses to answers on a separate survey that measured three dimensions of happiness: *enjoyment* ("My life is filled with pleasure"), *engagement* ("Most of the time, I am fascinated by what I am doing"), *meaning* ("I have a very clear idea about my purpose in life"), as well as symptoms of *depression* (e.g., "During the previous week, I had crying spells").

Among this sample, those who reported high levels of curiosity also reported high levels of pleasure, engagement, and meaning in their lives. Moreover, students with high levels of curiosity were also less likely to say they had felt depressed during the previous week. Correlation, of course, doesn't prove causation, so we shouldn't jump to conclude that curiosity wards off depression; it might work the other way around. Depression could, for example, inhibit curiosity; when we feel down, we may be less likely to pick up a book or explore our environment. The research team speculated that a more complex, perhaps symbiotic, relationship might be at play: When we're curious (and cultivate our curiosity), we may be more apt to seek new experiences, engage in new pursuits, and find deeper meaning in our lives. These dispositions may help us to "counteract the tendency to focus attention on negative aspects of life," which, when unchecked, can lead to or amplify depression (Kaczmarek et al., 2014). In other words, curiosity probably isn't a cure for acute depression, but it might offer a form or preventive medicine, making us less likely to sink into lethargy or despair.

USING CURIOSITY TO NAVIGATE EMOTIONAL CRISES

Curiosity also appears to help us navigate through emotional crises, which often force us to shift from one form of happiness to another. In midlife, for example, we may find that maintaining the physique we had as twentysomethings grows more difficult as our metabolism becomes less forgiving; thus, we find ourselves swearing off the foods and drink that once gave us pleasure (or consuming them with a side order of self-loathing).

Studies suggest, in fact, that many people—maybe even most of us—experience an emotional crisis at some point in our lives. A study of nearly 1,000 adults in the UK, for example, found that 22, 24, and 14 percent of people aged 20 to 39, 40 to 59, and over 60, respectively, reported being in a time of crisis—an emotionally volatile span that lasts a year or more and overwhelms their capacity to cope. During these crisis periods, they were left reexamining their lives and asking themselves soul-searching questions like, "Who am I, really?" (Robinson et al., 2016).

As noted earlier, young people today appear to be experiencing emotional crises at an alarming rate. According to recent data from the Centers for Disease Control (CDC, 2018), nearly one in three teens (31.5 percent) and two in five teenage girls (41.1 percent) experience "persistent feelings of sadness or hopelessness," and more than one in six (17.2 percent) have "seriously considered attempting suicide." In addition to smartphone use, a number of complex factors seem to be behind this rise in teenage depression, anxiety, and suicidal thoughts—including adverse childhood experiences to hypercompetitive schools and extracurricular activities that leave teens with little unstructured time to decompress and a persistent fear of failure.

No single strategy can help teens navigate or "snap out" of these emotional crises, of course. For teens swallowed up in deep depression, the best support we can offer is comprehensive mental health services. However, as we'll see, one of the most effective ways to help teens find their way out of a deep, dark hole of depression is to help them unleash a different kind of curiosity—a sort of *self-curiosity* that helps them to reexamine their own thoughts and recalibrate their personal formulas for happiness in order to arrive at newfound clarity, direction, and meaning for their lives.

In the next chapter, we'll see how, when channeled correctly, *reflective curiosity*—exploring our own beliefs, emotions, motivations, and aspirations—can lead to powerful realizations, insights, and meaning—both for ourselves and our students. By the same token, we'll also see how *too much* navel gazing can keep us from discovering what's often the shortest route to our happiness: getting outside of our own heads, taking a good look around, and seeing that what we need to be happy has often been right there in front of us all along.

A WONDERFUL LIFE

Most of us spend most of our waking hours tracking over pretty much the same ground—driving the same route to work, frequenting the same places, and taking our dog on the same loop through the neighborhood. So when we inadvertently take a wrong turn, we may suddenly find ourselves somewhere we've never been before—even if it's just one street off our normal route or a couple of blocks from home. At other times, a familiar place can suddenly look unfamiliar when viewed from a different side of the street, as if we're seeing it again for the first time. All these experiences may leave us wondering, *How have I never seen this place before*? We may also delight in a new discovery—like a new sidewalk café or a tree in bloom. As it turns out, the joy we find in making these small discoveries—closing knowledge gaps we didn't even know we had—can be therapeutic.

TAKE A LOOK AROUND . . . AND INSIDE

Years ago, a group of English therapists and researchers attempted to apply this concept in an unusual experiment with war veterans who were experiencing post-traumatic stress, children in poverty, and older adults suffering from memory loss. In a small yet in-depth study, they sought to help patients use curiosity to turn familiar places into unfamiliar ones, uncovering erstwhile unseen beauty in the world around them—and more contentment in themselves. Altogether, 27 people participated in the project, which was part of a larger, community-wide program called the Liverpool Decade of Health and Wellbeing, which encouraged people to, among other things, take notice of familiar places, seeing them through new eyes

(Phillips et al., 2015). The idea was to enable participants to create their own "therapeutic spaces" or settings that encourage rejuvenation. Typically, such places include forests, beaches, retreats, spas, and sacred places. For the Liverpool project, however, the goal was to help people turn their own urban environments into therapeutic spaces by seeing them in a new light—with *curiosity*—and in so doing, turn seemingly ordinary places into extraordinary ones. In short, they hoped to help people experience the same sense of well-being they might feel when admiring a mountain, studying a painting, or watching waves crash on the beach.

One such effort manifested as the Veterans' Photography project, which taught war survivors to think like photographers, capturing authentic glimpses of life, even in the mundane. For many of the ex-servicemen who entered the program encased in a shell of machismo, photography offered a safe way to express their emotions. One veteran, for example, photographed a picture of a tree growing out of a wall, which he found particularly poignant given his cancer diagnosis. Afterward, in discussion groups, as people talked about the photographs they'd taken, they offered a sort of "sideways mirror" for viewing their lives, giving them a way to step outside themselves and reflect on their own emotions and circumstances in a different light.

As photography made them more curious about the world around them, they also became more curious about their inner worlds. As one veteran put it, photography helped them search for the truth "no matter how shit the truth was." Thus, curiosity improved their well-being because it encouraged them to, in the words of the same veteran, stop "bottling up" things inside themselves because they were "too stubborn . . . to see another person's point of view." In many ways, curiosity—in this case, *reflective curiosity* about others' and their own feelings—offered a path out of the briar patch of their own tangled emotions and toward something resembling happiness.

USING CURIOSITY TO REEXAMINE OUR OWN "STINKING THINKING"

As any good therapist will tell you, the roots of unhappiness often lie in our own thoughts—what we tell ourselves about our own self-worth, how we interpret other's actions, and what we believe about the future. As University of Pennsylvania psychiatrist Aaron Beck (Beck et al., 1987) has noted, when we're depressed our thoughts often get lost inside something of a Bermuda Triangle of stinking thinking (what he calls a "cognitive triad" of depression) that consists of these three mutually reinforcing negative thoughts: "I'm no good," "My world is bleak," and "My future is hopeless."

Many of us may wrestle with one or two of these thoughts on occasion, yet before long, we can usually tamp them down. Depressed people, however, tend to hear all three thoughts playing in a near-constant loop in their minds. As a result, their thinking tends to fall into ruts or "cognitive distortions" that reinforce their negative feelings and perceptions. As popularized by David Burns (1989), here are some of these cognitive distortions (for a longer list with examples, see Tool 12: Show students how to dispel cognitive distortions with curiosity):

- Catastrophizing—focusing on the worst possible outcome

- Overgeneralizing—extrapolating a pattern from just one or two events

- Mind reading—making assumptions about others' motives

- Filtering—dwelling on negative events or details and ignoring positive ones

- Emotional reasoning—assuming our negative feelings reflect reality

Cognitive behavior therapy (CBT), which numerous studies have shown to be as effective as medication for addressing depression and suicidal thoughts (Spirito et al., 2011), teaches teens to reexamine their negative feelings by first identifying the event that triggered their negative thoughts and putting their feelings into words (e.g., No one liked my Instagram post, so I feel unpopular). Next, they surface the negative beliefs that led to those feelings (e.g., My friends didn't like my post because they think I'm unattractive). After that, they dispute those beliefs, typically by identifying the cognitive distortion at work (e.g., I'm mind reading, overgeneralizing, and filtering) and identifying alternative explanations (e.g., It was late at night when I posted so probably nobody saw it; and maybe I'm just oversensitive because I'm tired). Finally, they identify what *they* can do to change their negative thoughts (e.g.,

I'm going to remember my last post (it got dozens of likes), stop posting to Instagram at 2 a.m., and get more sleep).

Basically, CBT helps teens to engage in "Socratic questioning" of their own negative beliefs, asking themselves questions like, "Is this belief true?" "What is the evidence for this belief?" "Does this belief help me feel the way you want?" and "Is there another belief for this event?" (Spirito et al., 2011, p. 200). CBT isn't a cure-all, of course. Studies suggest that for severe cases of depression or suicide risk, CBT and medication *combined* are more powerful than either alone. Nonetheless, when we consider that questions are the heart of curiosity, encouraging students to embrace some *reflective curiosity* about their negative emotions, beliefs, and assumptions about others can help them find a way out of their own negative thoughts, anxieties, and feelings.

LOOKING IN ALL THE WRONG PLACES

That said, we're likely to encounter some limits, or at least diminishing returns, to our happiness if we focus solely on inner journeys of curiosity. In her book *America the Anxious: How Our Pursuit of Happiness Is Creating a Nation of Nervous Wrecks*, Ruth Whippman observes that Americans' obsession with happiness appears to have backfired. As a dour Brit transported to sunny California—where everyone around her seemed to expect to be happy (and fret something's wrong with them if they're not)—she finds it's odd how much Americans spend on self-help books and seminars to teach ourselves how to be happy while remaining so miserable (Whippman, 2016a).

One reason happiness may remain so elusive, she speculates, may simply be that the more we dwell on feeling happy, the less happy we feel. To wit: A study at the University of California, Berkeley invited two groups of people to report their happiness after watching a feel-good film. One group had previously read a short article on the importance of happiness; the other group read the same article with the words *accurate judgment* substituted for *happiness*. As it turned out, the group who *hadn't* read the article on happiness were more likely to report feeling positive emotions after the film, leading the researchers to conclude that "wanting to be happy may make people lonely" (Mauss et al., 2011). Or in

Whippman's (2016b) words, "Like an attractive man, it seems the more actively happiness is pursued, the more it refuses to call and starts avoiding you at parties."

LOOKING TO OTHERS

Another reason happiness may avoid us could be, as Whippman asserts, because we keep looking for it in the wrong places—namely, *inside* ourselves. Whether it's the perky social media memes (e.g., "Happiness is an inside job"), weekend journeys of self-discovery, or the uniquely American practice of cherishing "me time," we seem to have embraced a decidedly "isolationist" path to happiness (Whippman, 2017). As if we needed to spend more time alone. Already, Americans eat half of their meals by themselves, and as noted earlier, teens now spend less time hanging out with friends than any previous generation (NPD Group, 2014).

But the real shortcoming of an "isolationist" approach to happiness may be that it runs counter to what decades of research (and great literature) have shown: *Happiness depends on other people*—or more precisely, on helping other people. According to an exhaustive review of research by Richard Ryan and Edward Deci (2001)—two giants in the field of positive psychology—the factor most consistently linked to personal happiness is alternatively called *attachment* or *relatedness*; decades of research show relationship-enhancing personality traits consistently rank among the top attributes linked to well-being.

Not surprisingly, a Gallup worldwide survey of people's happiness discovered that individuals' well-being is strongly linked to the presence of social networks, which may explain why people in less well-to-do Latin American countries, like Guatemala, report, on average, greater day-to-day happiness than Americans (Gallup Organization, 2017). Introverts take heart: The *quantity* of social interactions isn't as important as the *quality* of those interactions; a study of 280 college students, for example, found happiness to be strongly correlated with friendship, even if students reported having just one best friend (Demir et al., 2007).

Perhaps most importantly, studies have found that engaging in small acts of kindness (e.g., helping a friend with schoolwork, visiting an elderly relative, writing a thank-you note) boost happiness

(Lyubomirsky et al., 2004). What this suggests is that the more we can nurture our curiosity for others—wondering about how to help people, connect with them, make the world around us a better place, and brighten someone else's day—the happier we're likely to be.

TURNING CURIOSITY INTO HAPPINESS

Let's take stock of what we've learned to ponder how we can help students translate curiosity into a greater sense of well-being and life satisfaction.

Musing #1: Find Your Wonder

A couple of years ago, while giving a talk about the power of curiosity to a group of statewide education leaders in Michigan, I had a brief but meaningful conversation during a break with then-state superintendent of schools, the late Brian Whiston. I shared with Whiston that my eldest daughter was enrolling in college but undecided as to her major. "Ask her what problem she wants to solve," he replied. I thought that was an interesting and compelling way to frame a college education—around curiosity. So I carried his advice back to her. As it turns out, his advice also reflects a key finding from Gallup's worldwide survey of happiness: Across the globe, on days when people feel happiest, it's often because they "learned something" the day before. Recall also that college students were happier and more energized on days when they were curious. In short, we are often happiest when we're learning—when we're pursuing knowledge that lies just over the horizon.

It's great to have professional pursuits around big, essential questions, but that's not always possible to do. Moreover, for students who are still trying to find their place in the world, encouragements (however well intentioned) to find and pursue their life's passion may seem like a bridge too far. The good news is that we can still feel energized and fulfilled by pursuing more simple questions—such as, How can I get better at chess? How do I grow vegetables in my yard? How can I teach my dog to catch a Frisbee? How can I talk to my teenager? (Or if you're a teen, how can I talk to my parents?) Basically, we're happier when we have mysteries—be they large or small—to pursue.

Musing #2: Stop, Look, and Listen

My grandmother was one of the happiest, most content people I've known. She lived on the same farm in Iowa her entire adult life. She probably spent 90 percent of her time in a one-square-mile area around the farmhouse, leaving only once a week or so for a pilgrimage to town to buy groceries, get her hair done, and run other errands.

In the twilight of her life, her daughters hoped she might move to town where she'd be safer, but she stayed put. Now I understand why. When I was in college, I exchanged monthly handwritten letters with her. Though her life seemed rather placid and simple to me, as I had ventured far from home to see the world, she could fill pages with descriptions of the changing seasons, migrating wildlife, and small happenings around the farm. Her small corner of the world was *always* changing and piquing her curiosity because she could appreciate the smallest of tiny details and thus see her surroundings anew every day—the flowers blooming, the birds at her window, the thunderheads forming across the cornfields.

Perhaps the most powerful insight to emerge from the Veterans' Photography project in Liverpool is that simply looking at things in a different light can make our familiar surroundings new again and provide us with small moments of joyful discovery. By using a photographer's eye to look more closely at places familiar to us, we're apt to see something new—a flowering tree, a beautiful sunset, a neighbor whose quiet kindness we view with admiration.

We can also listen closely, hearing sounds we've never noticed before, which, in turn, could leave us wondering, what's making that sound? A frog? A cricket? A locust? Where are they? If we allow ourselves to experience a childlike sense of wonder about the world around us, we can become everyday explorers constantly experiencing the joy of discovery.

Musing #3: Turn Negative Emotions and Experiences Into Questions

The first two musings reflect the power of being actively curious—asking questions and looking at the world around us through a lens of curiosity. Yet there's another powerful element of curiosity that's equally important to our happiness—something called *openness to experience*, or embracing novel experiences, engaging in personal growth, and responding to life's unexpected twists and turns with grace and humor (Malcolm, 2013). This form of curiosity, which reflects some of the key ideas from cognitive behavior therapy, can make even painful experiences more bearable when we we're able to say to ourselves, "OK, so that happened . . . what should I learn from that?" And "What might I be telling myself that's not only untrue but also contributing to my unhappiness?"

Viewing the vicissitudes of life with curiosity can also tamp down our anxieties about what may happen in the future because we figure, no matter the outcome, we'll pick ourselves up, dust ourselves off, and emerge a bit wiser. Reflecting upon his many studies of curiosity and happiness, Todd Kashdan, in fact, concluded that rolling with the punches may be *the key* to happiness as we encounter disappointments and uncertainties in our lives:

> We need to believe that we can handle that novelty and that uncertainty, and if we don't feel that we can handle it, we're not going to feel curious; we're going to feel confused or we're going to feel threatened. (Malcolm, 2013, para. 9)

HAPPINESS IS RIGHT UNDER OUR NOSES

Perhaps the most important lesson to draw from this research is that we're happiest when we're helping other people. As we've seen, on one level, curiosity can draw us closer to others, helping us learn what makes them tick and feeling compassion (or loving kindness) for them. Yet on a more sublime level, we might consider Aristotle's concept of *eudaemonia*—cultivating our virtues for the greater good—to contemplate what it would be like to cultivate our own *curiosity* for the greater good. On this level, curiosity is apt to deliver the greatest sense of fulfillment and meaning. We are not chasing horizons or pursuing questions for our *own* joy of discovery, but rather, we are looking to find answers that help others—for example, becoming a better parent, teacher, or coach; helping others work through their problems; or solving a vexing challenge for our colleagues, families, or students.

Chris McCandless appeared to have discovered this deep in the Alaska wilderness only after swearing off the typical hedonic pleasures of most young men his age—trading bars and pizza parlors for berries and small game—and immersing himself in the challenge of surviving in the wild. Could he have uncovered the same insight by staying at home and reading Tolstoy or the many studies cited here? Perhaps. Yet few of us learn life's lessons that way. Instead, we often must experience them and learn them ourselves. Only then do words jump off the pages of a book and speak to us—or does the advice of a loved one or friend resonate with us. In the end, perhaps only after exhausting the other forms of happiness could McCandless fully appreciate that the key to happiness lies in connecting with and helping other people. Sadly, his epiphany came too late, after he'd removed the guardrails from his life.

In many ways, McCandless's short life reflects curiosity burning brightly—an insatiable wanderlust entwined with dewy aspirations to emulate his hero, Henry David Thoreau, in living life to its fullest. We might see his tragic end as a cautionary tale about curiosity, the modern equivalent of Pandora or Eve. Yet for his biographer, Jon Krakauer, himself an avid mountaineer who understood the impulse to lead a life less ordinary, Chris's tragic story and sophomoric writings stirred not contempt, but compassion, as he saw in McCandless a portrait of himself as a young man.

If the studies of people in the UK are any indication, at some point in our lives most of us—and our students—will experience an emotional crisis when we wonder what it's all about and attempt (perhaps in less dramatic fashion) to chase horizons and escape a frenetic and callous society through some form of quietude and reflection where we hope to find the meaning of it all. It's in these times that curiosity can be a consort—helping us to reflect on our lives, wrestle with our negative emotions, dive deep into new experiences to escape a rut, find new joy in our surroundings, and perhaps, most importantly, reach out to, and connect with, people around us.

TOOLS TO SUPPORT CURIOUS WELL-BEING

Curiosity can be preventive medicine for mental health by helping us find the joy of discovery and productively question our own negative feelings and cognitive distortions. The strategies offered here—while no substitute for professional care for students facing serious mental health crises—are designed to help students translate curiosity into a greater well-being.

Tool 10: Create a Curiosity Journal

Key idea: Students can enhance their well-being and energy by nurturing their curiosity—finding ways to grow as a person, learning what captivates them, and solving mini-mysteries.

As we've seen, curiosity is linked to feeling more energetic, optimistic, and satisfied with our lives. We can encourage students to find a few small things each day to pique their curiosity. Students can record these ideas in a notebook, adding new entries and musings daily. Initially, they may be reluctant to share these episodes of curiosity—or not know where to look for them. So here are a few ways you can help them find sparks of curiosity:

- Look a little closer. Curiosity often starts with a mystery, which we can find all around us if we know where to look. Survey your surroundings until you see or hear something that perplexes you—a bird nest in a strange location, an ornately cut piece of wood, a pattern in people's behavior, a richly layered song, an engineering marvel, or an invention that leaves you wondering, How did that happen or how did people do that?

- Do self-improvement puzzles. We often have puzzles we're trying to solve for ourselves that begin with three simple words: *How do I . . .?* For example, how do I put more backspin on my basketball jump shot? How do I play that guitar riff? How do I get my dog to stop barking at strangers? How do I bake a tasty, gluten-free scone?

- Mash up ideas. Many great innovations—in arts, sports and leisure, technology, or business—reflect a mash up or fusion of seemingly unrelated ideas—such as mixing blues and country music, attaching a kite to a surfboard, putting a computer inside a music player, or retelling the classic literary epic in outer space. Try sparking your own curiosity by wondering what would happen if you mixed two seemingly incompatible ideas together—fusing genres in the arts, applying technology in a new area, or merging your two favorite but unrelated things.

- Consider what makes people (or groups) tick. Human beings are among the most fascinating things in the universe. No two of us are alike, so we all have individual quirks, anxieties, phobias, and personality traits that make us unique. Put us together in groups and our behavior is even more intriguing. What spark of curiosity do you feel about others—what do you want to know about why friends, family members, and groups behave the way they do? What makes one person so nice? And someone else so sullen? Why do individuals assume different personalities in groups?

- Ask deeper questions. Some of the best questions are those without answers—at least none you'll find in the back of a book, a Web search, or scientific experiment. These questions—about the meaning of life, your purpose in life, how the universe came into existence—fall into the realm of philosophy, religion, and metaphysics.

This is just a starter list. The point here is to encourage students to identify questions that keep them chasing horizons and looking forward to finding answers—and surfacing new questions.

Tool 11: Conduct an Interest Inventory

Key idea: Passion is key to persistence, yet for many young people, it's often easier to help them find interests that can grow into passions worthy of pursuit.

Beyond fleeting episodes of curiosity, students have greater well-being, goal orientation, and motivation when they have a *passion* worthy of pursuit that makes their lives meaningful. However, for many students, suggesting they find their life's passion can feel overwhelming, as they may not have sufficient interests to know what they're passionate about. So it's often easier to help them to identify things that hold their interest—areas they want to explore or master that provide the joy of discovery or moving closer to a goal. Over time, such interests can grow into passions worthy of pursuit. Here are questions to ask to help students identify their interests:

- What subjects or classes do you most enjoy in school?

- What topics/subjects/skills have you really enjoyed learning about in school?

- What skill have you taught yourself, on your own, outside of school?

- What was the last thing you felt curious enough about to investigate on your own?

- What kind of books/magazine articles/websites do you read for enjoyment?

- If you could ask a remarkable person for advice, who would it be? What would you ask?

- If you could plan a field trip to anywhere, where would you go? What would you learn?

- Which of these challenges do you find most engaging? Rank them in order from 1 to 7.

  - Figuring out how things work to fix them (e.g., electronics, cars, appliances)
  - Understanding what makes people tick—their motives, experiences, values
  - Engaging in creative, imaginative thinking (creating a story, song, recipe, etc.)
  - Helping others with problems (e.g., relationships, health, emotions, etc.)
  - Working with numbers/statistics to analyze information or solve problems
  - Practicing hard to get good at something
  - Exploring deep questions (e.g., about the universe, the meaning of life, society)

After students answer these questions, invite them to review their answers, looking for themes that reveal their natural curiosity—the things that make them curious, motivated, and excited to learn. Then, ask them write down three curiosity quests (areas, skills, challenges, mysteries, etc.) they'd like to explore in the next three months (and in so doing, experience joy and excitement).

Tool 12: Show Students How to Dispel Cognitive Distortions With Curiosity

Key idea: Bringing curiosity to our feelings helps us to dissect and "talk back" to the erroneous thinking that's often at the heart of our anxieties, negative feelings, and poor self-esteem.

Cognitive behavior therapy (CBT) can help people of all ages dissect their anxiety and depression by examining the exaggerated thoughts that create their negative feelings. By engaging in "Socratic questioning" of their troubling thoughts, students can begin to disentangle them and avoid negative feedback loops. Psychologists call these exaggerated and pernicious beliefs "cognitive distortions" and encourage teens to train themselves to recognize, refute, and replace them with more positive beliefs about themselves, others, and their futures. Here are 10 of the most common cognitive distortions adapted from the work of David Burns (1989):

- Catastrophizing—Focusing on the worst possible outcome (e.g., I didn't get a good score on my college entrance exam; looks like I'll be living in a van down by the river.)

- Emotional reasoning—Assuming one's negative emotions reflect reality (e.g., I feel insecure when she's talking to him; I bet she's going to dump me for him.)

- Filtering—Focusing only on negative events (e.g., That was awful; I missed a note.) and dismissing positive ones (e.g., People applauded, but they were just being nice.)

- Fortune telling—Making dire predictions with little evidence to support them (e.g., No one would go to prom with me; I'm going to wind up miserable and alone my whole life.)

- Labeling—Assigning blanket (negative) traits to entire groups of people (e.g., All football players are misogynists; people who drive pickup trucks are racists.)

- Mind reading—Making assumptions about others' motives (e.g., My sister borrowed my shirt because she thinks she looks prettier in it than I do.)

- Overgeneralizing—Extrapolating a general pattern from just one or two events (e.g., I got an F on the quiz because I'm dumb at math.)

- Personalizing—Taking things personally or blaming oneself for others' behaviors (e.g., He/she cheated on me because I'm not attractive.)

- Polarized thinking—Seeing the world in black/white, all/none, always/never terms with no gray areas (e.g., You're either with us or against us if you don't sign our petition.)

- "Should-y" thinking—Setting unrealistic expectations and beating ourselves up (or others) for not meeting them (e.g., I should stop eating ice cream late at night; I'm hopeless.)

Often, it's easier to identify others' faulty thinking than our own. So after you share and discuss this list with students, help them to find expressions of these distortions in literature, history, current events, and popular culture. Once they've identified the cognitive distortions (e.g., "labeling" in *Lord of the Flies*, "emotional reasoning" in *The Crucible* or Japanese internment camps, "polarized thinking" in McCarthyism or political debates, or "overgeneralizing" in people's prejudices, invite them to consider how refuting and replacing these distortions with more rational beliefs could create more positive outcomes. In doing so, students will begin to hear and avoid their own minds falling into these forms of exaggerated thinking.

Teaching about cognitive distortions is, of course, just one step toward better mental health and not a cure-all for mental health issues. Nonetheless, the more we can help students tamp down exaggerated, negative thinking and engage in positive self-talk, the more apt they'll be to emerge a bit stronger and wiser when they encounter life's inevitable setbacks and conflicts.

Becoming a Man (BAM): Helping Students Reexamine Their Thoughts to Prevent Violence

If only they'd paused to think about what they were doing for one second, things would be different. That's a common refrain often heard among incarcerated youth. "Very, very often, you know, if they could only take back five minutes of their life," notes Harold Pollack, a public health researcher at the University of Chicago Crime Lab, "a lot of these kids, a lot of the people that are locked up, would have a very different life" (Vedantam et al., 2017).

While poring over numerous case files of homicides in Chicago, Pollack and his research partner, Jens Ludwig, found that, contrary to popular perception, most were not premeditation, acts of revenge, or gang violence. Rather, they resulted from a perceived slight—a stolen coat, a hurled insult, a shoe being stepped on—escalating into murder. Pollack interviewed dozens of young men locked up for homicide and found many almost immediately regretted their actions, which led Pollack and Ludwig to a profound insight: Violent crimes are consistently the result of people acting without thinking—something not unique to young men on Chicago's South Side, of course. We all tend to act without thinking on occasion, yet in the world in which many of these young men live, the consequences of acting without thinking are often dire and irreversible.

That sparked Pollack and Ludwig to search for ways to help high school-aged men slow down their thinking and avoid taking regrettable actions, which led them to Youth Directions, a nonprofit that created a program called Becoming a Man (BAM)—a remarkably low-budget cognitive behavioral therapy intervention for high schoolers living in precarious circumstances (the program's participants live in dire poverty, have a D average in school, live in Chicago's most troubled housing projects, and fully 40 percent of them have been incarcerated).

A reporter from National Public Radio visited a routine, monthly meeting of the BAM program in one such school, Orr High, a hulking building that sits largely empty as nearby families have fled the troubled school in droves. Shortly after noon, 11 young men filed into the room, sat down, and began their usual "check-in" process, sharing how they feel physically, intellectually, emotionally, and spiritually. One young man shared he felt exhausted from a late-night job; another was anxious about an upcoming test. After a lengthy round of sharing, the young men engaged in trust-building exercises before diving into a group therapy session to discuss real-life scenarios and how they might respond, not with actions first, but thinking.

Over the course of several sessions, the young men began to see their automatic thoughts were often exaggerated and erroneous—that is, cognitive distortions. For instance, as one young man explained to a reporter (Vedantam et al., 2018), before entering the program he'd gotten into a fight at school because he believed, erroneously, he was attacking a boy who'd stolen his jacket. He's now able to pause a beat, reflect on his own thoughts, and allow his own cooler thinking to prevail. For example, when

(Continued)

(Continued)

he saw another boy talking to his girlfriend, he initially felt enraged as he assumed the boy was disrespecting him, essentially telling him he wasn't man enough to keep his girl. But thanks to what he'd learned in group therapy, he paused a moment to examine the thought and realize it might be erroneous. So instead of getting in a fight, he talked to the other boy and learned he and his girlfriend were just having a friendly conversation.

A randomized control study of the Becoming a Man program (Heller et al., 2017) found promising results—including a 28 to 35 percent drop in arrest rates and a 45 to 50 percent drop in arrests for violent crimes for young men in the program compared with a control group not in the program; on top of that, youth participating in the program were more likely to attend school, pass their classes, and stay in school—results the researchers attributed not only to improving their emotional intelligence, social skills, grit, or self-control, but also simply, "helping youth slow down and reflect on whether their automatic thoughts and behaviors are well suited to the situation they are in, or whether the situation should be construed differently" (p. 2).

In short, by learning to reexamine their own thinking—having brief sparks of curiosity about their own assumptions, which, in turn, create space for them to consider alternate explanations—these young men are able to do what few other programs or approaches have done, helping them avoid lethal conflicts and incarceration.

STANDING AT
A CURIOUS
CROSSROADS

Don't let anyone rob you of your imagination, your creativity, or your curiosity. It's your place in the world; it's your life. Go on and do all you can with it and make it the life you want to live.

—Mae Jemison

We're all born curious. It's what makes us human—the desire to explore, to learn, and to connect with other people. It's deeply embedded in all of us. Yet some of our present troubles—such as the ones that follow—suggest we may be running out of curiosity, as individuals, educators, schools, and a society:

- Twenty years of heavy-handed reforms narrowly focused on standardized achievement tests have left many students disengaged and educators dispirited, feeling incurious.

- In many organizations and schools, the key driver of continuous improvement and innovation—honest reflection and asking "what-if" questions about possibilities—becomes replaced with incurious groupthink that avoids examining assumptions and, as a result, often leads to finger pointing and declining performance.

- Authentic interpersonal bonds and compassionate concern and curiosity for others appear to have withered in our digitally connected society in which many people—of all ages—are "alone together."

- Depression, substance abuse, and teen suicide rates are all on the rise for reasons that appear to include people lacking interpersonal connections, meaningful intellectual pursuits, and the ability to engage in reflective curiosity, reexamining the exaggerated beliefs at the root of their unhappiness.

This book invites us all to consider a larger, what-if question—namely, what if we could help our students and ourselves nurture the natural curiosity that's inside all of us, waiting to come out? What might be different in our classrooms? Our schools? For our students? Their relationships? The organizations they will someday enter and lead? And what might be different for us as a society if we were all just a little more curious about one another and the world around us?

DO WE REALLY HAVE TIME FOR CURIOSITY?

It's likely, though, that despite all of these possibilities, some school and district leaders and community members may dismiss curiosity as a nicety, but not a necessity—something far down their list of concerns, seemingly less important than raising student achievement on standardized tests, addressing students' social-emotional or mental health issues, or ensuring their safety from school shootings. For some leaders, especially those in disadvantaged communities that face these and many other stark, everyday challenges, attending to a "nicety" like curiosity may seem hopelessly irrelevant, naïve, or quixotic.

I've occasionally had some well-meaning leaders ask me, in fact, whether any of this curiosity stuff is relevant for *all* kids, especially those who might be wondering where they'll find their next meal, bed, or caretaker. What use do *they* have for curiosity? For that matter, what use do families who are wondering how to stretch their paychecks through the end of the month while keeping their kids clothed and fed have for curiosity? Isn't all of this curiosity talk just a "white privilege" thing?

I certainly hope not.

In fact, I'd ask this question: Given all we know about the power of curiosity to support student success in learning, life, relationships, and well-being, don't *all kids* deserve to be curious?

Moreover, as researchers (e.g., Darling-Hammond, 2007) have found, it's often black, brown, and impoverished children who are most apt to experience blighted approaches to teaching and suffer through a scripted, narrow curriculum focused on low-level, recognition, and recall learning for standardized tests. As a result, children of color often find themselves in bleak, soulless places where they sit in straight rows, walk in silence in hallways, and engage in rote learning with little room for curiosity, creativity, or compassion. And we act surprised and dismayed when they drop out of those learning environments at higher rates than kids in more affluent schools.

EVERY KID DESERVES A CURIOUS SCHOOL

In his book *The Trouble With Black Boys: And Other Reflections on Race, Equity, and the Future of Public Education*, UCLA professor Pedro Noguera (2009) urges us to move past polarized academic debates that frame achievement gaps as either a function of institutionalized racism limiting students' opportunities or a culture of poverty that deters students from accessing opportunities. Noguera dismisses this as a false dichotomy and argues that achievement gaps are likely the result of *both* as well as what lies deep inside students themselves.

Yes, inequitable institutional barriers hinder students' success, and cultural influences can instill counterproductive attitudes about schooling. Individuals aren't powerless in the face of institutions nor are they "hopelessly trapped within a particular social and cultural milieu" (Noguera, 2009, p. 25). Rather, they can exercise "individual choice and agency" to overcome both institutional and cultural hindrances (p. 25). Nonetheless, for many students individual agency alone often isn't enough to overcome institutional hurdles and cultural drag chutes. So Noguera urges that we focus on *all three* forces—institutional, cultural, and individual—something we can do as educators by creating curious schools. Doing so can, for example, remove institutional impediments to student success by ensuring all students benefit from teachers who are curious about them, curious about their profession, and curious about the subjects they teach. We can also support students with positive *cultural* forces that embrace curiosity thinking, positive attitudes about learning, and compassionate curiosity for one another. Finally, by giving students opportunities to pursue their own interests and engage in reflective curiosity, we can help them develop the individual passion and persistence they need to succeed in school and beyond.

Or we could set all of that aside and persist with a meager focus on prepping students for tests and moving "bubble kids" from one performance band to the next, creating places where students are disengaged, disenchanted, and disconnected and likely acting out as a result. In short, we could keep doing the same things and hope for different results.

But in light of all the positive things curiosity pulls into its orbit, we might wonder, What if we could ensure *all kids* experience a curious school—one that unleashes their talents, compassion, happiness, and opportunities for success? The power is in our hands. We can change our schools and the lives of our students for the better. All it might take is for everyone in a school to rekindle our sense of wonder about our students, our profession, and to consider *what if* students could experience the joy of curiosity in every class, every day?

IMAGINE ALL THE (CURIOUS) PEOPLE

Imagine for a moment what it might look like if we did that— if we shifted our conversations in school board meetings, faculty lounges, and school parking lots away from preconceived notions of what's *not* possible and instead engaged in shared explorations of *what ifs*. Imagine what new possibilities for the future might spring out of curiosity. We might be able to

- Reimagine our schools as places where students can develop their intellectual curiosity to become scientists, entrepreneurs, inventors, caregivers, and real-world problem solvers.

- Help students cultivate interpersonal curiosity to become compassionate citizens who seek to understand one another, solve problems together, and give back to their communities.

- Create schools where teachers feel encouraged to be professionally curious; experience the joy of tapping into their own intellectual curiosity about teaching, learning, and supporting students to create innovations; discover better ways of working together as professionals to learn together; and help one another get a little better every day.

- Encourage students to put down their phones and just talk to one another, with no tweets, likes, or pins—just meaningful questions that go beyond the superficial to find real connections and compassion for others. In so doing, they might begin to appreciate one another in new ways and see there's more that unites us as human beings than divides us.

- Help our youth become curious people, using curiosity to navigate the challenges of life while finding greater purpose and meaning in their lives.

IT ALL STARTS WITH A SPARK

Take heart: Curiosity needn't be a grandiose life decision; it can be quite simple and personal, bubbling up from within us. Yes, people can trigger or stifle our curiosity, but ultimately, being curious is a choice we can make every day for ourselves.

We can wake up and decide we already know everything there is to know, that we have all the right answers, and there's nothing new to experience, no one new to meet, no new places to go, and no new discoveries to make. In short, we can decide to live a life without surprises, hemmed in by the familiar, the certain, and the ordinary. We can choose—as individuals or as an entire school—to be *incurious*, living a humdrum, predictable existence in the shadowed vale of what we already know or think we know.

Or we can decide that today and hereafter we'll wake up curious, priming our brains for learning and opening our minds to new possibilities. We can decide to search for new answers, explore new places (even if it's just a different street on our way home from work), and get to know one new person a little better. We can emerge from the shadows of the predictable, mundane, and familiar, climb a hill and search for something that lies just beyond our horizon—be it physical, intellectual, interpersonal, or introspective. And we can share that joy of discovery with our students.

In the end, the most important and encouraging thing about curiosity is that it's already within all of our students, waiting to be unleashed. Though others may suppress it, it's still there, like a cork held underwater, waiting to pop back to the surface as soon as we release it again. Being a curious person need not be a chore or something we must work assiduously to develop; rather, a person should become curious in small and simple ways, following one question after another, like a string of lamps lighting our way through the darkness.

So with that in mind, I leave you to wonder and wander with one final question: What are you curious about now?

REFERENCES

Ainsworth, M. D. S., Blehar, M. C., Waters, E., & Wall, S. N. (2015). *Patterns of attachment: A psychological study of the strange situation.* Psychology Press.

American Federation of Teachers [AFT]. (2017). *2017 educator quality of work life survey.* Author.

Anderson, M., & Jiang, J. (2018). *Teens, social media and technology 2018.* Pew Research Center.

Anwar, Y. (2015, February 12). *Creating love in the lab: The 36 questions that spark intimacy.* Berkeley News. http://news.berkeley.edu/2015/02/12/love-in-the-lab/

Aron, A., Melinat, E., Aron, E., Vallone, R. D., & Bastor, R. J. (1997). The experimental generation of interpersonal closeness: A procedure and some preliminary findings. *Personality and Social Psychology Bulletin, 23*(4), 363–377.

Aron, A. R., Shohamy, D., Clark, J., Myers, C., Gluck, M. A., & Poldrack, R. A. (2004). Human midbrain sensitivity to cognitive feedback and uncertainty during classification learning. *Journal of Neurophysiology, 92*(2), 1144–1152.

Aron, E. (2015, March 18). *Thirty-six questions for intimacy, back story.* Huffington Post. https://www.huffingtonpost.com/elaine-aron-phd/36-questions-for-intimacy_b_6472282.html

Baker, D. A., & Algorta, G. P. (2016). The relationship between online social networking and depression: A systematic review of quantitative studies. *Cyberpsychology, Behavior, and Social Networking, 19*(11), 638–648.

Barker, J. E., Semenov, A. D., Michaelson, L., Provan, L. S., Snyder, H. R., & Munakata, Y. (2014). Less-structured time in children's daily lives predicts self-directed executive functioning. *Frontiers in Psychology, 5*(593). https://www.frontiersin.org/articles/10.3389/fpsyg.2014.00593/full

Barnwell, P. (2014, April 22). *My students don't know how to have a conversation.* The Atlantic. https://www.theatlantic.com/education/archive/2014/04/my-students-dont-know-how-to-have-a-conversation/360993/

Batson, C. D. (2009). These things called empathy: Eight related but distinct phenomena. In J. Decety & W. Ickes (Eds.), *The social neuroscience of empathy* (pp. 3–15). MIT Press.

Beck, A. T., Rush, A. J., Shaw, B. F., & Emery, G. (1987). *Cognitive therapy of depression.* Guilford Press.

Berdik, C. (2014). *A different abstinence education.* Slate. https://slate.com/technology/2015/06/disconnect-project-teenagers-give-up-smartphones-for-a-week.html

Berger, W. (2015, September 11). *Why curious people are destined for the C-suite.* Harvard Business Review. https://hbr.org/2015/09/why-curious-people-are-destined-for-the-c-suite

Berliner, D. C., & Biddle, B. J. (1995). *The manufactured crisis: Myths, fraud, and the attack on America's public schools.* Addison-Wesley.

Bill & Melinda Gates Foundation. (2015). *Teachers know best: Making data work for teachers and students.* Author.

Black, J. S., & Gregersen, H. B. (2014). *It starts with one: Changing individuals changes organizations.* Pearson Education.

Boone, C., De Brabander, B., & Hellemans, J. (2000). Research note: CEO locus of control and small firm performance. *Organization Studies, 21*(3), 641–646.

Bridgeland, J. M., DiIulio, J., & Morison, K. B. (2006). *The silent epidemic: Perspectives of high school dropouts.* Civic Enterprises.

Bronson, P., & Merryman, A. (2010, July 10). The creativity crisis. *Newsweek.* www.newsweek.com/2010/07/10/the-creativity-crisis.html

Bryk, A. S., Gomez, L. M., Grunow, A., & LeMahieu, P. (2015). *Learning to improve: How America's schools can get better at getting better.* Harvard Education Press.

Burns, D. (1989). *The feeling good handbook.* HarperCollins.

Busteed, B. (2013, January 7). *The school cliff: Student engagement drops with each school year.* Gallup Organization. https://news.gallup.com/opinion/gallup/170525/school-cliff-student-engagement-drops-school-year.aspx

Cain, S. (2013). *Quiet: The power of introverts in a world that can't stop talking.* Random House.

Carson, C. C., Huelskamp, R. M., & Woodall, T. D. (1992). Perspectives on education in America: An annotated briefing. *Journal of Educational Research, 86*(5), 259–310.

Catron, M. L. (2015, January 11). To fall in love with anyone, do this. *The New York Times.* https://www.nytimes.com/2015/01/11/fashion/modern-love-to-fall-in-love-with-anyone-do-this.html

Celik, P., Storme, M., Davila, A., & Myszkowski, N. (2016). Work-related curiosity positively predicts worker innovation. *Journal of Management Development, 35*(9), 1184–1194.

Centers for Disease Control. (2018). *Prescription opioid overdose data.* https://www.cdc.gov/drugoverdose/data/overdose.html

Cigna. (2018, May 1). *New Cigna study reveals loneliness at epidemic levels in America.* https://www.cigna.com/newsroom/news-releases/2018/pdf/new-cigna-study-reveals-loneliness-at-epidemic-levels-in-america.pdf

Clawson, L. (2012, March 4). *New York City's flawed data fuel Right's war on teachers.* Daily Kos. https://www.dailykos.com/story/2012/30/04/1069927/-New-York-City-s-flawed-data-fuels-the-right-s-war-on-teachers

Cobb, P., Boufi, A., McClain, K., & Whitenack, J. (1997). Reflective discourse and collective reflection. *Journal for Research in Mathematics Education, 28*(3), 258–277.

Collins, J. (2009). *How the mighty fall: And why some companies never give in.* HarperCollins.

Covey, S. (1989). *The 7 habits of highly effective people: Powerful lessons in personal change.* Simon & Schuster.

Csikszentmihalyi, M., Rathunde, K., & Whalen, S. (1993). *Talented teenagers: The roots of success and failure.* Cambridge University Press.

Cushman, K. (2010). *Fires in the mind: What kids can tell us about motivation and mastery.* Jossey-Bass.

Darling-Hammond, L. (2007). Race, inequality and educational accountability: The irony of "No Child Left Behind." *Race, Ethnicity and Education, 10*(3), 245–260.

Datnow, A., Park, V., & Kennedy-Lewis, B. (2013). Affordances and constraints in the context of teacher collaboration for the purpose of data use. *Journal of Educational Administration, 51*(3), 341–362.

Dean, C., Hubbell, E., Pitler, H., & Stone, B. (2012). *Classroom instruction that works: Research-based strategies for increasing student achievement* (2nd ed.). ASCD.

Demir, M., Özdemir, M., & Weitekamp, L. A. (2007). Looking to happy tomorrows with friends: Best and close friendships as they predict happiness. *Journal of Happiness Studies, 8*, 243–271.

Demonte, J. (2017). *Micro-credentials for teachers: What three early adopter states have learned so far.* American Institutes for Research.

Deutschman, A. (2006). *Change or die: Three keys to change at work and in life.* Harper Business.

Diener, E., & Biswas-Diener, R. (2002). Will money increase subjective well-being? *Social Indicators Research, 57*(2), 119–169.

Ehrenreich, B. (1985, February 21). Hers. *The New York Times.* http://www.nytimes.com/1985/02/21/garden/hers.html

Endsley, R. C., Hutcherson, M. A., Garner, A. P., & Martin, M. J. (1979). Interrelationships among selected maternal behaviors, authoritarianism, and preschool children's verbal and nonverbal curiosity. *Child Development, 50*(2), 331–339.

Engel, S. (2011). Children's need to know: Curiosity in schools. *Harvard Educational Review, 81*(4), 625–645.

Engel, S. (2015a). *The hungry mind: The origins of curiosity in childhood*. Harvard University Press.

Engel, S. (2015b). *Over-testing kids is not the answer: Here's how we really spark curiosity*. Salon. https://www.salon.com/2015/03/14/over_testing_kids_is_not_the_answer_heres_how_we_really_spark_creativity/

Engel, S., & Randall, K. (2009). How teachers respond to children's inquiry. *American Educational Research Journal, 46*(1), 183–202.

Engelhard, G. (1985). *The discovery of educational goals and outcomes: A view of the latent curriculum of schooling*. Unpublished doctoral dissertation. University of Chicago.

Engelhard, G., & Monsaas, J. A. (1988). Grade level, gender and school-related curiosity in urban elementary schools. *Journal of Educational Research, 82*(1), 22–26.

Escueta, M., Quan, V., Nickow, A. J., & Oreopoulos, P. (2017). *Education technology: An evidence-based review* (No. w23744). National Bureau of Economic Research.

Fernández-Aráoz, C. (2014). 21st century talent spotting. *Harvard Business Review, 92*(6), 46–56. https://hbr.org/2014/06/21st-century-talent-spotting

First Round Review. (n.d.). *Hire a top performer every time with these interview questions*. http://firstround.com/review/hire-a-top-performer-every-time-with-these-interview-questions/

Fischer, P., Krueger, J. I., Greitemeyer, T., Vogrincic, C., Kastenmüller, A., Frey, D., Heene, M., Wicher, M., & Kainbacher, M. (2011). The bystander-effect: A meta-analytic review on bystander intervention in dangerous and non-dangerous emergencies. *Psychological Bulletin, 137*(4), 517.

Fredericksen, B. L., Cohn, M. A., Coffey, K. A., Pek, J., & Finkel, S. M. (2008). Open hearts build lives: Positive emotions, induced through loving-kindness meditation, build consequential resources. *Journal of Personal Social Psychology, 95*, 1045–1062.

Friedman, T. L. (2005, April 3). It's a flat world, after all. *The New York Times*. https://www.nytimes.com/2005/04/03/magazine/its-a-flat-world-after-all.html?_r=0

Gaffigan, J. (2013). *Dad is fat*. Three Rivers Press.

Gallup Organization. (2017). *Gallup 2017 Global Emotions*. Author.

Gansberg, M. (1964, March 27). Thirty-seven who saw murder didn't call the police. *The New York Times*. https://www.nytimes.com/1964/03/27/37-who-saw-murder-didnt-call-the-police.html

Garrosa, E., Blanco-Donoso, L. M., Carmona-Cobo, I., & Moreno-Jimenez, B. (2016). How do curiosity, meaning in life, and search for meaning predict college students' daily emotional exhaustion and engagement? *Journal of Happiness Studies, 18*(1), 1–24.

Giambra, L. M., Camp, C. J., & Grodsky, A. (1992). Curiosity and stimulation seeking across the adult life span: Cross-sectional and 6-to 8-year longitudinal findings. *Psychology and Aging, 7*(1), 150.

Goddard, R., Goddard, Y., Sook Kim, E., & Miller, R. (2015). A theoretical and empirical analysis of the roles of instructional leadership, teacher collaboration, and collective efficacy beliefs in support of student learning. *American Journal of Education, 121*(4), 501–530.

Goertzel, T. (2004). Cradles of eminence—then and now. *Parenting for High Potential.* https://www.questia.com/magazine/1P3-741068721/cradles-of-eminence-then-and-now

Goertzel, V., Goertzel, M. G., Goertzel, T. G., & Hansen, A. (2004). *Cradles of eminence: Childhoods of more than 700 famous men and women.* Gifted Psychology Press.

Good, T. L., Slavings, R. L., Harel, K. H., & Emerson, H. (1987). Student passivity: A study of question asking in K-12 classrooms. *Sociology of Education, 60,* 181–199.

Goodman, J. (2012). *Gold standards? State standards reform and student achievement.* Program on Education Policy and Governance, Harvard University. https://www.hks.harvard.edu/pepg/ PDF/Papers/PEPG12-05

Goodwin, B. (2003, December). *Digging deeper: Where does the public stand on standards-based education?* McREL International.

Goodwin, B. (2015). Getting unstuck. *Educational Leadership, 72,* 8–12.

Goodwin, B., Rouleau, K., & Lewis, D. (2017). *Curiosity works: A guidebook for moving your school from improvement to innovation.* McREL International.

Gottfried, A. E., Fleming, J., & Gottfried, A. W. (2001). Continuity of academic intrinsic motivation from childhood through late adolescence: A longitudinal study. *Journal of Educational Psychology, 93*(1), 3–13.

Gray, L., & Taie, S. (2015). *Public school teacher attrition and mobility in the first five years: Results from the first through fifth waves of the 2007–08 beginning teacher longitudinal study* (NCES 2015-337). U.S. Department of Education. National Center for Education Statistics. http://nces.ed.gov/pubsearch

Grazioplene, R. G., DeYoung, C. G., Rogosch, F. A., & Cicchetti, D. (2013). A novel differential susceptibility gene: CHRNA4 and moderation of the effect of maltreatment on child personality. *Journal of Child Psychology and Psychiatry, 54(8),* 872–880.

Greenfield, P. M. (2012). The changing psychology of culture from 1800 to 2000. *Psychological Science,* 24(9), 1722–1731.

Grove, A. (2010). *Only the paranoid survive: How to exploit the crisis points that challenge every company.* Random House.

Gruber, M. J., Gelman, B. D., & Ranganath, C. (2014). States of curiosity modulate hippocampus-dependent learning via the dopaminergic circuit. *Neuron,* 84(2), 486–496.

Hacker, A. (2012, July 29). Is algebra necessary? *The New York Times*. https://www.nytimes.com/2012/07/29/opinion/sunday/is-algebra-necessary.html

Hardy, J. H., Ness, A. M., & Mecca, J. (2017). Outside the box: Epistemic curiosity as a predictor of creative problem solving and creative performance. *Personality and Individual Differences, 104*, 230–237.

Heller, S. B., Shah, A. K., Guryan, J., Ludwig, J., Mullainathan, S., & Pollack, H. A. (2017). Thinking, fast and slow? Some field experiments to reduce crime and dropout in Chicago. *Quarterly Journal of Economics, 132*(1), 1–54.

Henderson, B., & Moore, S. G. (1980). Children's responses to objects differing in novelty in relation to level of curiosity and adult behavior. *Child Development, 51*(2), 457–465.

Herold, B. (2016, January 13). Unleashing classroom analytics. *Education Week*, S2–7.

Heshmat, S. (2015, January 22). The addictive quality of curiosity: Curiosity as an antidote to boredom and addiction. *Psychology Today*. https://www.psychologytoday.com/blog/science-choice/201501/the-addictive-quality-curiosity

Holt-Lunstand, J., Smith, T. B., & Layton, J. B. (2010). Social relationships and mortality risk: A meta-analytic review. *PLOS Medicine, 7*(7). http://journals.plos.org/plosmedicine/article?id=10.1371/journal.pmed.1000316

Horn, I. S., Kane, B. D., & Wilson, J. (2015). Making sense of student performance data: Data use logics and mathematics teachers' learning opportunities. *American Educational Research Journal, 52*(2), 208–242.

Hsee, C., & Ruan, B. (2015). Curiosity kills the cat. In K. Diehl & C. Yoon (Eds.), *Advances in consumer research* (pp. 63–64). Association for Consumer Research.

Hsee, C., Ruan, B., & Lu, Z. Y. (2015). Creating happiness by first inducing and then satisfying a desire: The case of curiosity. In K. Diehl & C. Yoon (Eds.), *Advances in consumer research* (pp. 287–291. Association for Consumer Research.

Hsee, C. K., & Ruan, B. (2016). The Pandora effect: The power and peril of curiosity. *Psychological Science, 27*(5), 659–666.

IHI Multimedia Team. (2015). Like magic? ("Every system is perfectly designed. . ."). http://www.ihi.org/communities/blogs/origin-of-every-system-is-perfectly-designed-quote

Ingersoll, R. M., Merrill, E., Stuckey, D., & Collins, G. (2018). *Seven trends: The transformation of the teaching force–updated October 2018*. Consortium for Policy Research in Education.

Isaacson, W. (2007). Twenty things you need to know about Albert Einstein. *Time*. http://content.time.com/time/specials/packages/article/0,28804,1936731_1936743_1936745,00.html

Johnson, S. M., Kraft, M. A., & Papay, J. P. (2012). How context matters in high-need schools: The effects of teachers' working conditions on their professional satisfaction and their students' achievement. *Teachers College Record, 114*(10), 1–39.

Jones, M. G. (1990). Action zone theory, target students and science classroom interactions. *Journal of Research in Science Teaching, 27*(8), 651–660.

Kaczmarek, L., Baczkowski, B., Enko, J., Baran, B., & Theuns, P. (2014). Subjective well-being as a mediator for curiosity and depression. *Polish Psychological Bulletin, 45*(2), 200–204.

Kagan, J. (1989). Temperamental contributions to social behavior. *American Psychologist, 44*, 668–674.

Kahneman, D. (2011). *Thinking, fast and slow*. Farrar, Straus & Giroux.

Kahneman, D., & Deaton, A. (2010). High income improves evaluation of life but not emotional well-being. *Proceedings of the National Academies of Sciences, 107*(38), 16489–16493.

Kang, M. J., Hsu, M., Krajbich, I. M., Loewenstein, G., McClure, S. M., Wang, J. T. Y., & Camerer, C. F. (2009). The wick in the candle of learning: Epistemic curiosity activates reward circuitry and enhances memory. *Psychological Science, 20*(8), 963–973.

Kashdan, T. B., McKnight, P. E., Fincham, F. D., & Rose, P. (2011). When curiosity breeds intimacy: Taking advantage of intimacy opportunities and transforming boring conversations. *Journal of Personality, 79*(6), 1369–1401.

Kashdan, T. B., & Roberts, J. (2004). Trait and state curiosity in the genesis of intimacy: Differentiation from related constructs. *Journal of Social and Clinical Psychology, 23*(6), 792–816.

Kashdan, T. B., & Steger, M. (2007). Curiosity and pathways to well-being and meaning in life: Traits, states, and everyday behaviors. *Motivation and Emotion, 31*(3), 159–173.

Kashdan, T., Stiksma, M. C., Disabato, D. J., McKnight, P. E., Bekier, J., Kaji, J., & Lazarus, R. (2018). The five-dimensional curiosity scale: Capturing the bandwidth of curiosity and identifying four unique subgroups of curious people. *Journal of Research in Personality, 73*, 130–149.

Kelly, S., & Turner, J. (2009). Rethinking the effects of classroom activity structure on the engagement of low-achieving students. *Teachers College Record, 111*(7), 1665–1692.

Konrath, S. H., O'Brien, E. H., & Hsing, C. (2011). Changes in dispositional empathy in American college students over time: A meta-analysis. *Personality and Social Psychology Review, 15*(2), 180–198.

Krakauer, J. (1996). *Into the Wild*. Anchor Books.

Labi, A. (2014). *Closing the skills gap: Companies and colleges collaborating for change*. https://www.luminafoundation.org/files/publications/Closing_the_skills_gap.pdf

Larson, L. R., & Lovelace, M. D. (2013). Evaluating the efficacy of questioning strategies in lecture-based classroom environments: Are we asking the right questions? *Journal on Excellence in College Teaching, 24*(1), 105–122.

Lazarín, M. (2014). *Testing overload in America's schools.* Center for American Progress.

Levin, T., & Long, R. (1981). *Effective instruction.* ASCD.

Levitt, S. D., List, J. A., Neckerman, S., & Sadoff, S. (2012). *The behavioralist goes to school: Leveraging behavioral economics to improve educational performance* (NBER Working Paper Series No. 18165). National Bureau of Economic Research.

Loewenstein, G. (1994). The psychology of curiosity: A review and reinterpretation. *Psychology Bulletin, 116*(1), 75–98.

Louv, R. (2008). *Last child in the woods: Saving our children from nature-deficit disorder.* Algonquin Books.

Lowry, N., & Johnson, D. W. (1981). Effects of controversy on epistemic curiosity, achievement, and attitudes. *Journal of Social Psychology, 115*, 31–43.

Luscombe, B. (2018, October 4). Bob Iger's bets are paying off big time for Disney. *Time.* https://time.com/magazine/south-pacific/5415167/october-15th-2018-vol-192-no-15-international/

Lyubomirsky, S., Tkach, C., & Sheldon, K. M. (2004). *Pursuing sustained happiness through random acts of kindness and counting one's blessings: Tests of two six-week interventions.* Unpublished data, Department of Psychology, University of California, Riverside.

Maheady, L., Mallette, B., Harper, G. F., & Sacca, K. (1991). Heads together: A peer-mediated option for improving the academic achievement of heterogeneous learning groups. *Remedial and Special Education, 12*(2), 25–33.

Malcolm, L. (2013). Does curiosity trump happiness in the wellbeing stakes? *Australian Broadcasting Corporation.* http://www.abc.net.au/radionational/programs/allinthemind/curiosity/4692056

Marzano, R., & Kendall, J. (1998). *Awash in a sea of standards.* McREL.

Marzano, R. J., Waters, T., & McNulty, B. A. (2005). *School leadership that works: From research to results.* ASCD.

Mauss, I. B., Savino, N. S., Anderson, C. L., Weisbuch, M., Tamir, M., & Laudenslager, M. L. (2011). The pursuit of happiness can be lonely. *Emotion, 12*(5), 908–912.

McFeely, S. (2018). *Why your best teachers are leaving and 4 ways to keep them.* Gallup Organization. https://www.gallup.com/education/237275/why-best-teachers-leaving-ways-keep.aspx

McMahan, E. A., & Estes, D. (2011). Hedonic versus eudaimonic conceptions of well-being: Evidence of differential associations with self-reported well-being. *Social Indicators Research, 103*(1), 93–108.

Medina, J. (2008). *Brain rules: Twelve principles for surviving and thriving at work, home, and school.* Pear Press.

Merry, S. (2016, June 29). Her shocking murder became the stuff of legend. But everyone got the story wrong. *The Washington Post.* https://www.washingtonpost.com/lifestyle/style/her-shocking-murder-became-the-stuff-of-legend-but-everyone-got-the-story-wrong/2016/06/29/544916d8-3952-11e6-9ccd-d6005beac8b3_story.html?utm_term=.5c913f83b59f

MetLife. (2013). *The MetLife survey of the American teacher: Challenges for school leadership.* https://www.metlife.com/content/dam/microsites/about/corporate-profile/MetLife-Teacher-Survey-2012.pdf

Meyer, K. (2014, February 6). How to hire curious people and keep curiosity alive. *Forbes.* https://www.forbes.com/sites/85broads/2014/02/06/how-to-hire-curious-people-and-keep-curiosity-alive/#6cb78e0794e3

Minor, D., Brook, P., & Bernoff, J. (2017, December 28). *Are innovative companies more profitable?* MITSloan Management Review. https://sloanreview.mit.edu/article/are-innovative-companies-more-profitable/

Moore, S. G., & Bulbulian, K. N. (1976). The effects of contrasting styles of adult–child interaction on children's curiosity. *Developmental Psychology, 12*(2), 171–172.

Munafò, M. R., Yalcin, B., Willis-Owen, S. A., & Flint, J. (2008). Association of the dopamine D4 receptor (DRD4) gene and approach-related personality traits: Meta-analysis and new data. *Biological Psychiatry, 63*(2), 197–206.

Munro, J. (2015). *Curiouser and curiouser.* McREL International.

Mussel, P. (2012). Introducing the construct curiosity for predicting job performance. *Journal of Organizational Behavior, 34,* 453–472.

National Commission on Excellence in Education. (1983, April). *A nation at risk: The imperative for educational reform.* https://www2.ed.gov/pubs/NatAtRisk/index.html

National Park Service. (n.d.). *The life of Theodore Roosevelt.* https://www.nps.gov/thri/theodorerooseveltbio.htm

National Research Council. (2011). *Successful K–12 STEM education: Identifying effective approaches in science, technology, engineering, and mathematics.* The National Academies Press.

Neumann, M., Edelhäuser, F., Tauschel, D., Fischer, M. R., Wirtz, M., Woopen, C., Haramati, A., & Scheffer, C. (2011). Empathy decline and its reasons: A systematic review of studies with medical students and residents. *Academic Medicine, 86*(8), 996–1009.

Noguera, P. A. (2009). *The trouble with black boys: And other reflections on race, equity, and the future of public education.* John Wiley & Sons.

NPD Group. (2014, August 6). *Consumers are alone over half of eating occasions as a result of changing lifestyles and more single-person households, reports NPD.* https://www.npd.com/wps/portal/npd/us/ news/press-releases/consumers-are-alone-over-half-of-eating-occa sions-as-a-result-of-changing-lifestyles-and-more-single-person-house holds-reports-npd

Olds, J., & Schwartz, R. (2009). *The lonely American: Drifting apart in the 21st century.* Beacon Press.

Organisation for Economic Cooperation and Development (OECD). (2011). *Strong performers and successful reformers in education: Lessons from PISA for the United States.* https://www.oecd.org/ dataoecd/32/50/46623978.pdf

Patall, E., Cooper, H., & Robinson, J. C. (2008). The effects of choice on intrinsic motivation and related outcomes: A meta-analysis of research findings. *Psychological Bulletin, 134*(2), 270–300.

Peljko, Z., Jeraj, M., Săvoiu, G., & Marič, M. (2017). An empirical study of the relationship between entrepreneurial curiosity and innovative-ness. *Organizacija, 49*(3), 172–182.

Peterson, C., Ruch, W., Beermann, U., Park, N., & Seligman, M. E. P. (2007). Strengths of character, orientations to happiness, and life sat-isfaction. *The Journal of Positive Psychology, 2*(3), 149–156.

Phillips, R., Evans, B., & Muirhead, S. (2015). Curiosity, place, and well-being: Encouraging place-specific curiosity as a "way to well-being." *Environment and Planning, 47*(11), 2339–2354.

Pianta, R. C., Belsky, J., Houts, R., & Morrison, F. (2007). Opportuni-ties to learn in America's elementary classrooms. *Science, 315*(5820), 1795–1796.

Queensland College of Teachers. (n.d.). *Teacher stories: Pasi Sahlberg.* Author. http://stories.qct.edu.au/pasi-sahlberg.html

Raine, A., Reynolds, C., Venables, P. H., & Mednick, S. A. (2002). Stim-ulation seeking and intelligence: A prospective longitudinal study. *Journal of Personality and Social Psychology, 82*(4), 663–674.

Reio, T. G., & Wiswell, A. (2000). Field investigation of the relationship among adult curiosity, workplace learning, and job performance. *Human Resource Development Quarterly, 11*(1), 5–30.

Richardson, M., Abraham, C., & Bond, R. (2012). Psychological cor-relates of university students' academic performance: A systematic review and meta-analysis. *Psychological Bulletin, 138*(2), 353–387.

Rideout, V. (2018). *The Common Sense census: Media use by tweens and teens.* Common Sense.

Rivers, J., Mullis, A. K., Fortner, L. A., & Mullis, R. L. (2012). Rela-tionships between parenting styles and the academic performance of adolescents. *Journal of Family Social Work, 15*(3), 202–216.

Robinson, O., Demetre, J. D., & Litman, J. A. (2016). Adult life stage and crisis as predictors of curiosity and authenticity: Testing inferences from Erikson's lifespan theory. *International Journal of Behavioral Development, 41*(3), 1–6.

Rowe, M. B. (1986). Wait time: Slowing down may be a way of speeding up! *Journal of Teacher Education, 37*(1), 43–50.

Ryan, R. M., & Deci, E. (2001). On happiness and human potentials: A review of research on hedonic and eudaimonic well-being. *Annual Review of Psychology, 52*, 141–166.

Sachs, J. (2017). Restoring American happiness. In J. Helliwell, R. Layard, & J. Sachs (Eds.), *World happiness report*. Sustainable Development Solutions Network.

Sahlberg, P. (2011). *Finnish lessons: What can the world learn from educational change in Finland?* Teachers' College Press.

Sahlberg, P. (2018). *FinnishED leadership: Four big, inexpensive ideas to transform education*. Corwin.

Sanders, T., & Palka, M. K. (2009, May 3). Students taking advanced placement have tripled in Duval County, but more fail. *Jacksonville Times Union*.

Satell, G. (2014, September 5). A look back at why Blockbuster really failed and why it didn't have to. *Forbes*. https://www.forbes.com/sites/gregsatell/2014/09/05/a-look-back-at-why-blockbuster-really-failed-and-why-it-didnt-have-to/#15127de41d64

Schmidt, F., & Hunter, J. (1998). The validity and utility of selection methods in personnel psychology: Practical and theoretical implications of 85 years of research findings. *Psychological Bulletin, 124*(2), 262–274.

Schochet, P. Z., & Chiang, H. S. (2010). *Error rates in measuring teacher and school performance based on student test score gains* (NCEE 2010–4004). National Center for Education Evaluation and Regional Assistance, Institute of Education Sciences, U.S. Department of Education.

Schulman, M. (2002). The passion to know: A developmental perspective. In C. R. Snyder & S. J. Lopez (Eds.), *The handbook of positive psychology* (pp. 313–327). Oxford University Press.

Schulz, L., & Bonawitz, E. (2007). Serious fun: Preschoolers engage in more exploratory play when evidence is confounded. *Developmental Psychology, 43*(4), 1045–1050.

Segal, N. (2000). *Entwined lives: Twins and what they tell us about human behavior*. Plume.

Shah, P. E., Weeks, H. M., Richards, B., & Kaciroti, N. (2018). Early childhood curiosity and kindergarten reading and math academic achievement. *Pediatric Research, 84*(3), 380–386.

Shaw, L. (2006, November 5). Foundation's small-schools experiment has yet to yield big results. *The Seattle Times*. http://old.seattletimes.com/html/education/2003348701_gates05m.html

Sherman, E. (2015, September 30). America is the richest, and most unequal, country. *Forbes*. http://fortune.com/2015/09/30/america-wealth-inequality/

Singer, T., & Klimecki, O. M. (2014). Empathy and compassion. *Current Biology, 24*(18), R875–R878.

Smith, T. (2014, March 17). *Does teaching kids to get "gritty" help them get ahead?* National Public Radio. http://www.npr.org/sections/ed/2014/03/17/290089998/does-teaching-kids-to-get-gritty-help-them-get-ahead

Spirito, A., Esposito-Smythers, C., Wolff, J., & Uhl, K. (2011). Cognitive-behavioral therapy for adolescent depression and suicidality. *Child and Adolescent Psychiatric Clinics of North America, 20*(2), 191–204.

Stanovich, K. E. (1986). Matthew effects in reading: Some consequences of individual differences in the acquisition of literacy. *Reading Research Quarterly, 21*(4), 360–406.

Steblay, N. M. (1987). Helping behavior in rural and urban environments: A meta-analysis. *Psychological Bulletin, 102*(3), 346–356.

Steger, M. (2010, June 3). The good from the bad: The full life is a blend of the good and the bad. *Psychology Today.* https://www.psychologytoday.com/us/blog/the-meaning-in-life/201006/the-good-the-bad

Steger, M. F., Hicks, B. M., Kashdan, T. B., Krueger, R. F., & Bouchard, T. J. (2007). Genetic and environmental influences on the positive traits of the values in action classification, and biometric covariance with normal personality. *Journal of Research in Personality, 41*(3), 524–539.

Stigler, J. W., & Hiebert, J. (2004). Improving mathematics teaching. *Educational Leadership, 61*(5), 12–17.

Strauss, V. (2015, June 12). Why so many teachers leave—and how to get them to stay. *The Washington Post.* https://www.washingtonpost.com/news/answer-sheet/wp/2015/06/12/why-so-many-teachers-leave-and-how-to-get-them-to-stay/? utm_term=.f701f59b92f3

Stringer, K. (2019). *Curriculum designer Christina Riley teaches students compassion and empathy alongside literacy. Here's how she does it.* The 74. https://www.the74million.org/article/74-interview-curriculum-designer-christina-riley-teaches-students-compassion-and-empathy-alongside-literacy-heres-how-she-does-it/

Subotnik, R. F., Tai, R. H., & Almarode, J. (2011, May 10–12). *Study of the impact of selective SMT high schools: Reflections on learners gifted and motivated in science and mathematics.* Paper prepared for the workshop of the Committee on Highly Successful Schools or Programs for K–12 STEM Education, National Research Council, Washington, DC.

Swan, G. E., & Carmelli, D. (1996). Curiosity and mortality in aging adults: A 5-year follow-up of the western collaborative group study. *Psychology and Aging, 11*(3), 449–453.

Torrance, P. E. (1963). The creative personality and the ideal pupil. *Teachers College Record, 65*(3) 220–226.

Torrance, P. E. (1965). *Rewarding creative behavior: Experiments in classroom creative behavior.* Prentice Hall.

Turkle, S. (2012, April 21). The flight from conversation. *The New York Times.* https://www.nytimes.com/2012/04/22/opinion/sunday/the-flight-from-conversation.html

Turkle, S. (2015, September 27). Stop Googling. Let's talk. *The New York Times.* http://www.nytimes.com/2015/09/27/opinion/sunday/stop-googling-lets-talk.html?_r=0

Twenge, J. (2018). *iGen: Why today's super-connected kids are growing up less rebellious, more tolerant, less happy—and completely unprepared for adulthood.* Simon & Schuster.

Twenge, J. M., Joiner, T. E., Rogers, M. L., & Martin, G. N. (2018). Increases in depressive symptoms, suicide-related outcomes, and suicide rates among US adolescents after 2010 and links to increased new media screen time. *Clinical Psychological Science, 6*(1), 3–17.

Tyre, P. (2016). The math revolution. *The Atlantic.* https://www.theatlantic.com/magazine/archive/2016/03/the-math-revolution/426855/

Uhls, Y. T., Michikyan, M., Morris, J., Garcia, D., Small, G. W., Zgourou, E., & Greenfield, P. M. (2014). Five days at outdoor education camp without screens improves preteen skills with nonverbal emotion cues. *Computers in Human Behavior, 39*(October), 387–392.

van Schijndel, T. J. P., Franse, R. K., & Raijmakers, M. E. J. (2010). The exploratory behavior scale: Assessing young visitors' hands-on behavior in science museums. *Science Education, 94*(5), 794–809.

Vedantam, S., Penman, M., Schmidt, J., Boyle, T., Klahr, R. Cohen, R., & Connelly, C. (2017, February 21). *On the knife's edge: Using therapy to address violence among teens.* National Public Radio. https://www.npr.org/2017/02/21/512035150/on-the-knifes-edge-using-therapy-to-address-violence-among-teens

Victoria State Government. (2018). *2017 annual report to the school community: School name—Glenroy Central Primary School.* Author. https://www.glenroycentralps.vic.edu.au/uploaded_files/media/annual_report_.pdf

Wallace, J. C., Little, L. M., Hill, A. D., & Ridge, J. W. (2010). CEO regulatory foci, environmental dynamism, and small firm performance. *Journal of Small Business Management, 48*(4), 580–604.

Walsh, J. A., & Sattes, B. D. (2016). *Quality questioning: Research-based practice to engage every learner* (2nd ed.). Corwin.

Warren, T. (2013, November 12). *Microsoft axes its controversial employee ranking system.* The Verge. https://www.theverge.com/2013/11/12/5094864/microsoft-kills-stack-ranking-internal-structure

Whippman, R. (2016a). *America the anxious: How our pursuit of happiness is creating a nation of nervous wrecks.* St. Martin's Press.

Whippman, R. (2016b, December 22). *America is obsessed with happiness—and it's making us miserable.* Vox. https://www.vox.com/first-person/2016/10/4/13093380/happiness-america-ruth-whippman

Whippman, R. (2017, October 27). Happiness is other people. *The New York Times.* https://www.nytimes.com/2017/10/27/opinion/sunday/happiness-is-other-people.html

Whyte, W. (1952). Groupthink. *Fortune.* http://fortune.com/2012/07/22/groupthink-fortune-1952/

Williams, C. (2018). The perks of a play-in-the-mud educational philosophy. *The Atlantic.* https://www.theatlantic.com/education/archive/2018/04/early-childhood-outdoor-education/558959/

Winerip, M. (2011, March 6). Evaluating New York teachers: Perhaps the numbers do lie. *The New York Times.* https://www.nytimes.com/2011/03/07/education/07winerip.html

Yazzie-Mintz, E. (2010). *Charting the path from engagement to achievement: A report on the 2009 High School Survey of Student Engagement.* Center for Evaluation & Education.

Young, V. M., House, A., Wang, H., Singleton, C., & Klopfenstein, K. (2011). *Inclusive STEM schools: Early promise in Texas and unanswered questions.* National Research Council.

Index

Noguera, Pedro A., 167–168
Nokia, 67–68, 82–83
Novelty
    chemical reactions in brain,
        25–26
    openness to, 9, 15, 155–156
Numbered heads together
    approach, 52

Olds, Jaqueline, 116
Openness to experience, 9, 15,
    155–156
Outdoors play, 53, 54

Parents
    expectations of schools, 47
    promoting curiosity in children,
        19–20
    secure attachment, 16, 51
Personality traits
    happiness and, 145–146, 153
    positive and negative affect,
        122, 123
    social anxiety, 122
    See also Interpersonal curiosity;
        Trait curiosity
Perspective taking, 108, 109,
    131–132
Pew Research Center, 110
Plato, *Allegory of the Cave*, 27
Play. See Outdoors play
Pollack, Harold, 162–163
Positive psychology, 46, 153
    See also Happiness
Principals
    coaching skills, 71
    leadership, 79–80, 92–93, 95
    See also Leaders

Questions
    of children, 3–4
    deep, 51
    directed, 51–52
    encouraging intimacy,
        117–120, 121, 126–127

inquiry-driven learning, 99–101
interpersonal curiosity
    experiment, 121–123
    leading with, 94–95
    thought-provoking, 52, 62–64
    waiting for answers, 52–53
    "what if," 91–93

Randall, Kellie, 43–44
Reflective curiosity, 148, 150,
    152, 169
Revolving-door thinking, 93–94
Riley, Christine, 134
Roberts, John, 121–123
Roosevelt, Eleanor, xxii, 19, 50
Roosevelt, Theodore, 19, 50, 53
Rowe, Mary Budd, 52–53
Ruan, Bowen, 141–142
Ryan, Richard M., 153

Sahlberg, Pasi, 81–83, 87–88
Schools
    collective efficacy, 91
    data availability and use,
        87–88, 90–91
    data teams, 71–72, 79–80, 91
    organizational cultures, 77–78,
        79, 96, 169
    performance pressures,
        37–43, 46
    principals, 71, 79–80,
        92–93, 95
    See also Classrooms; Education
        reform; Teachers
Schwartz, Richard, 116
Science
    controversies, 60–61
    investigations, 48–50
    standardized test scores, 56
    See also STEM education
Secrets, 8
Secure attachment, 16, 51
Self-curiosity. See Reflective
    curiosity
Small data, 88

Smartphones
  cultural impact, 110–112,
    115–116
  effects on interpersonal
    relationships, 111–112,
    113–116, 119–120,
    125–126
  happiness and, 111
  mental health impact,
    111, 116, 130, 148
  quitting cold turkey,
    113–114, 115
  taking breaks from, 126,
    129–131, 169
  See also Social media
Social anxiety, 122
Social media
  taking breaks from, 113–114,
    125–126, 129–131, 169
  use by teenagers, 110–112, 116
  See also Smartphones
Social relationships. *See*
    Interpersonal relationships
Societal change. *See* Cultural
    change
Solutionitis, 70–71
Southwest Airlines, 92
Specific curiosity, 6–7
Square, 92
Standardized tests, 37, 38–42,
    49, 56
Standards, 37–38, 40, 43, 47
State curiosity, 9, 10,
    122–123, 145
Steger, Michael, 143–144
Stein, Ben, 34, 51
STEM education, 55–58
  See also Mathematics; Science
"Stinking thinking, 150–152
Strangers, 105–108, 123
Students. *See* Classrooms;
    Teenagers
Substance abuse, 26, 166
Suspense, 59, 60
Swan, Gary E., xxi–xxii

Talmud, Max, 53
Teachers
  attitudes toward curiosity,
    43–44
  behaviors promoting curiosity,
    18–19
  boring, 34–35
  coaching and feedback, 71,
    77, 101
  data teams, 71–72
  hiring, 80–83, 84
  inquiry-driven learning, 99–101
  micro-credentialing, 42
  modeling curiosity, 46–47,
    168–170
  moral purposes, 96–98
  performance ratings, 39, 42,
    43, 46, 70–71
  professional development, 42,
    99–100
  questions asked, 51–53,
    62–64
  retaining, 71, 77–78
  stress, 43
  value placed on curiosity,
    33–34, 46
  See also Classrooms; Schools
Teach for America, 93
Teams. *See* Data teams; Work
    teams
Technology. *See* Smartphones;
    STEM education
Teenagers
  attitude changes, 109–111
  Becoming a Man program,
    162–164
  depression, 110, 111, 147–148,
    151–152, 166
  drivers, 111
  emotional crises, 147–148
  engagement in school, 32–33,
    46–47
  high school yearbook paradox,
    32–33
  robotics competition, 55

Leadership That Makes an Impact

**MICHAEL FULLAN &
MARY JEAN GALLAGHER**

With the goal of transforming the culture of learning to develop greater equity, excellence, and student well-being, this book will help you liberate the system and maintain focus.

PETER M. DEWITT

This step-by-step how-to guide presents the six driving forces of instructional leadership within a multistage model for implementation, delivering lasting improvement through small collaborative changes.

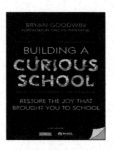

BRYAN GOODWIN

If you've ever wondered anything, really—just out of curiosity—then you have what it takes to lead your school from restored curiosity and your students to well-being and success.

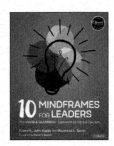

**JOHN HATTIE &
RAYMOND L. SMITH**

Based on the most current Visible Learning® research with contributions from education thought leaders around the world, this book includes practical ideas for leaders to implement high-impact strategies to strengthen entire school cultures and advocate for all students.

**DAVIS CAMPBELL &
MICHAEL FULLAN**

The model outlined in this book develops a systems approach to governing local schools collaboratively to become exemplars of highly effective decision-making, leadership, and action.

**MICHAEL FULLAN,
JOANNE QUINN, &
JOANNE MCEACHEN**

The comprehensive strategy of deep learning incorporates practical tools and processes to engage educational stakeholders in new partnerships, mobilize whole-system change, and transform learning for all students.

**JOANNE QUINN,
JOANNE MCEACHEN,
MICHAEL FULLAN,
MAG GARDNER, &
MAX DRUMMY**

Dive into deep learning with this hands-on guide to creating learning experiences that give purpose, unleash student potential, and transform not only learning, but life itself.

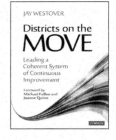

JAY WESTOVER

The transformative framework outlined in this book creates a districtwide approach for changing the culture of learning and creating a coherent system of continuous improvement.

ANTHONY KIM, KEARA MASCARENAZ, & KAWAI LAI

This guide provides battle-tested practices to help leaders build better habits for team learning, meetings, and projects, to achieve a more responsive, innovative organization.

EVAN ROBB

Build the foundations of effective leadership despite daily distractions. Learn how to intentionally use ten-minute opportunities to consider and execute your vision.

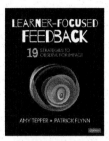

AMY TEPPER & PATRICK FLYNN

Nineteen strategies help leaders, coaches, and teachers improve their ability to identify desired outcomes, recognize learning in action, collect relevant evidence, and develop effective feedback.

JULIE M. WILSON

Learn to make sense of challenging change journeys and accelerate implementation with this practical framework that includes human-centered tools, resources, and mini case studies.

GRANT LICHTMAN

Our rapidly evolving world is dramatically impacting how we view schools. *Thrive* shows educators how they can help their schools not only survive but thrive during rapid change.

ERIC SHENINGER

The future-forward framework in this book prepares leaders to harness the power of innovative ideas and digital strategies to create relevant, engaging, and intuitive school cultures.

CHRISTINE MASON, PAUL LIABENOW, & MELISSA PATSCHKE

Envision and enact transformative change with an iterative visioning process, thought-provoking vignettes, case studies from exemplary schools, key strategies and tools, and practical implementation ideas.

KIRSTEN RICHERT, JEFFREY IKLER, & MARGARET ZACCHEI

Shifting empowers educational change leaders to proactively and coherently navigate complex, unprecedented change in schools and establish a school culture in which changemakers can thrive.

A SAGE Publishing Company

Helping educators make the greatest impact

CORWIN HAS ONE MISSION: to enhance education through intentional professional learning.

We build long-term relationships with our authors, educators, clients, and associations who partner with us to develop and continuously improve the best evidence-based practices that establish and support lifelong learning.

INTERNATIONAL

About McREL International

McREL is a non-profit, non-partisan education research and development organization that helps educators flourish by turning knowledge about what works in education into practical, effective resources and services for teachers and school leaders across the U.S. and around the world.